Pen & Pixel Fusion Volume 1

Triple Time

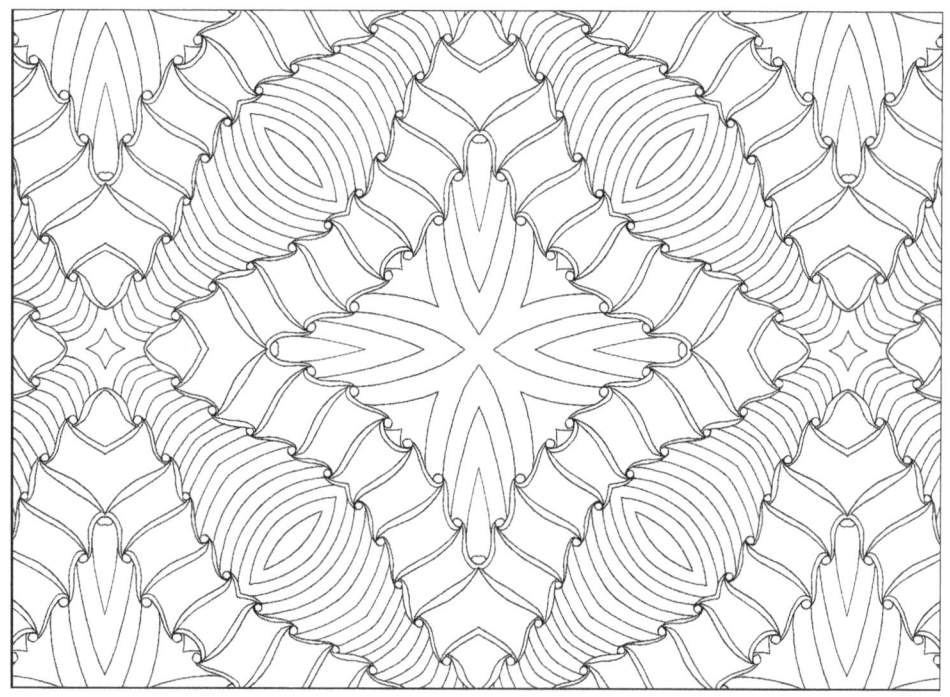

Written and Illustrated by Tina Golden

Printed in the United States of America

First Printing, 2015

ISBN-10: 1518836224
ISBN-13: 978-1518836220

Tina Golden
Doodletime Designs
16 Maple Street
Augusta, ME 04330

http://www.DoodletimeDesigns.com

Thank you for purchasing Triple Time, the first volume of the Pen & Pixel Fusion grown-up coloring book series.

There is a running debate among artists and colorists as to which is better, hand-drawn work or digital art. I say, why choose just one? It's the artist's imagination and creativity that makes something art, not the tools they use to do it.

In that spirit, I decided to embrace the wide variety of digital tools available to enhance and transform my original hand-drawn work. The Pen & Pixel Fusion series was born from that embrace and I think you're going to love it just as much as I do.

Within Triple Time, you will first find 15 of my original hand-drawn designs. These have simply been converted to high quality digital images and cleaned up a bit. You'll see all the weebles, wobbles, and other imperfections that you'll find in hand-drawn art.

Next, there are 15 beautiful, intricate mandalas created by digitally manipulating the original designs. You get all the soul of the hand-drawn art but the perfect symmetry only achieved through software.

Last, but not least, there are 15 relaxing pattern pages that were also created by digitally manipulating the original pieces. Pattern pages are one of the most soothing types of coloring pages, as most have repetitive motifs which can be quite meditative to the colorist.

With Pen & Pixel Fusion, you get the best of both worlds. Every line on every design has been lovingly hand-drawn to create this unique coloring book. I hope you enjoy coloring it as much as I enjoyed crafting it for you.

Tips for coloring the images in Triple Time

Let me start by saying there is no wrong way to color. It is supposed to be fun, creative, and relaxing. It's not very relaxing to have negative thoughts or get anxious over how your picture is turning out. Take a deep breath, let go of any negativity, and just be in the moment while you color these designs.

Coloring is a great way to release your inner creativity. A lot of people find that coloring inspires them to be creative in other areas of their lives, so when you're feeling stuck about something – color!

I recommend colored pencils or other dry media with this book, but you can use other media such as gel pens or markers if you take some care. Wet media can bleed through the pages onto another design. To avoid that, make sure to put an extra sheet of paper or card-stock behind the page you're coloring. There are three extra blank sheets at the back of the book that you can use for this purpose if you don't have card-stock handy.

If there is an image that you really want to turn out a certain way, feel free to photocopy the image onto the paper of your choice. I find a light-weight card stock perfect for my own coloring. It holds up nicely to markers and gel pens, but has enough tooth to work great with colored pencils, as well.

Photocopying your favorite designs can really allow you to relax and go with the flow when coloring as it takes all the worry out of it. It's an automatic do-over because you still have the original to print another. It's also a great way to try a different coloring palette.

I enjoy seeing how other people color my designs and learning about their techniques, so I'd love to have you share any finished pieces on my Facebook page or tag me on any social media channels we're both on. And both authors and artists thrive on reviews so please help me out by posting a review on Amazon – your support will enable me to keep bringing you new and exciting coloring books.

See you there!

Tina Golden

Connect With Me:

Website: http://www.DoodletimeDesigns.com

Facebook: https://www.facebook.com/DoodletimeOriginals

Twitter: https://twitter.com/ArtByTinaGolden

Pinterest: https://www.pinterest.com/tmgenterprises/

Google+: http://bit.ly/20KIPBP

YouTube: http://bit.ly/1MytwWO

Amazon: http://www.amazon.com/author/tinagolden

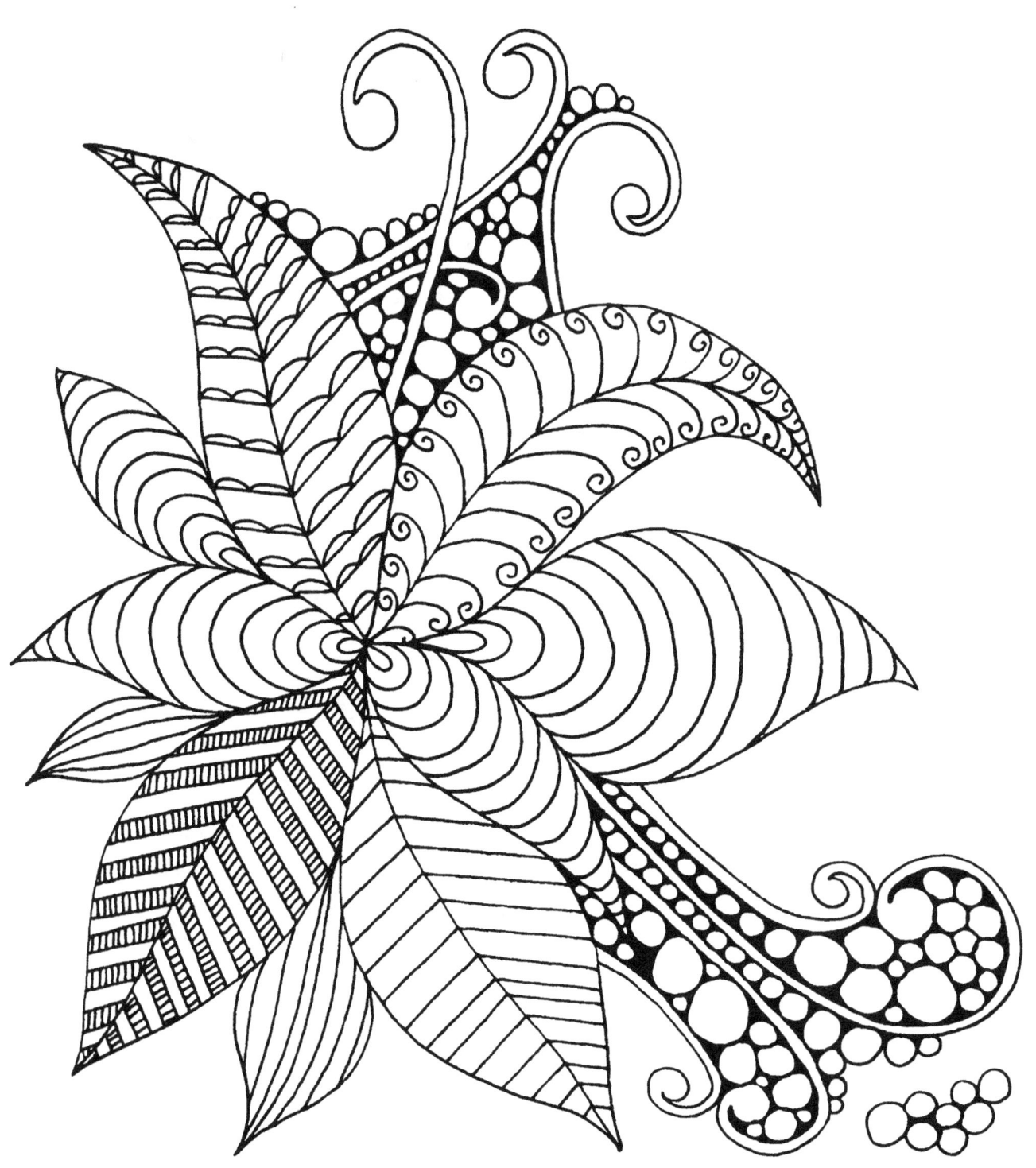

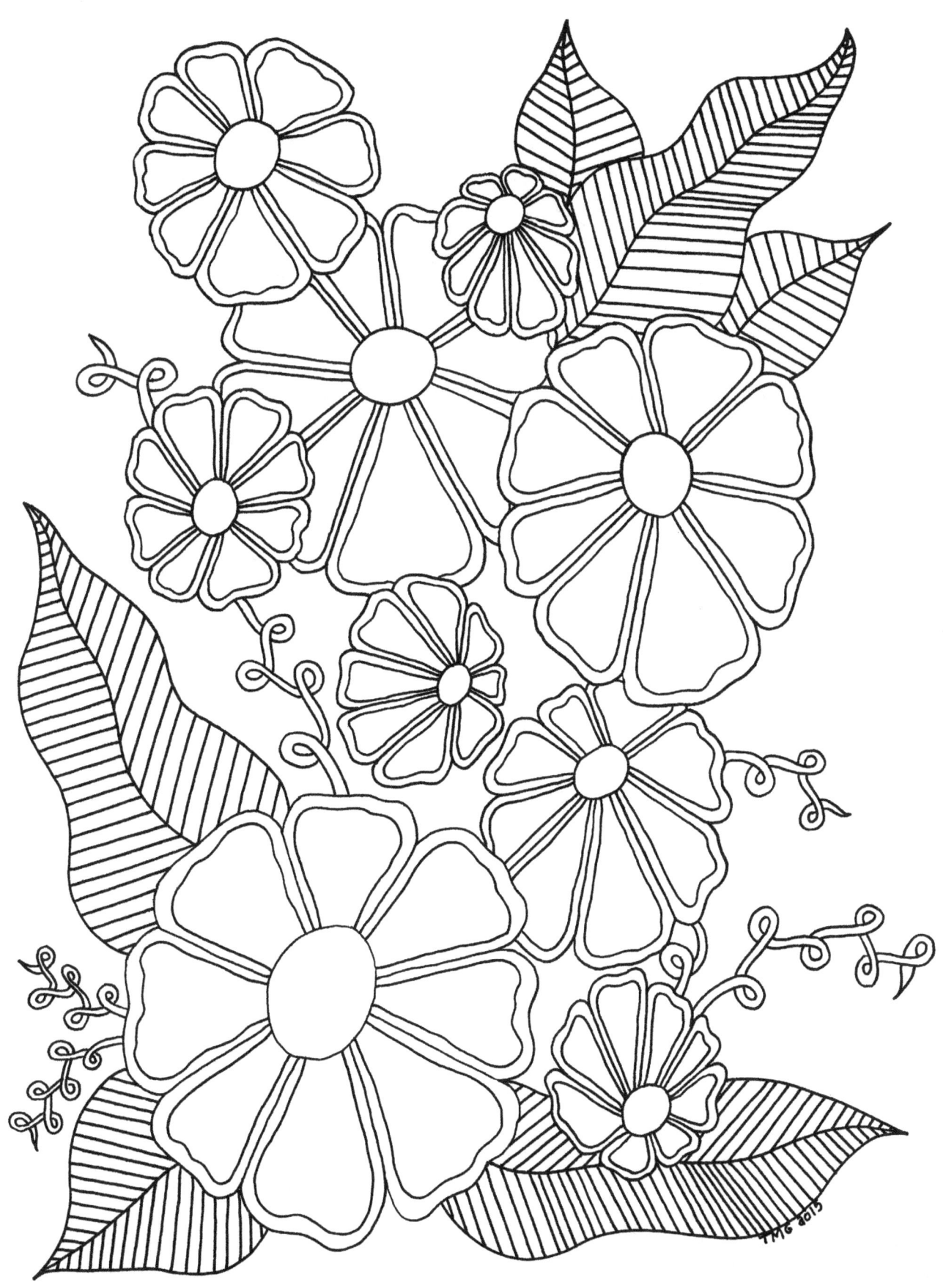

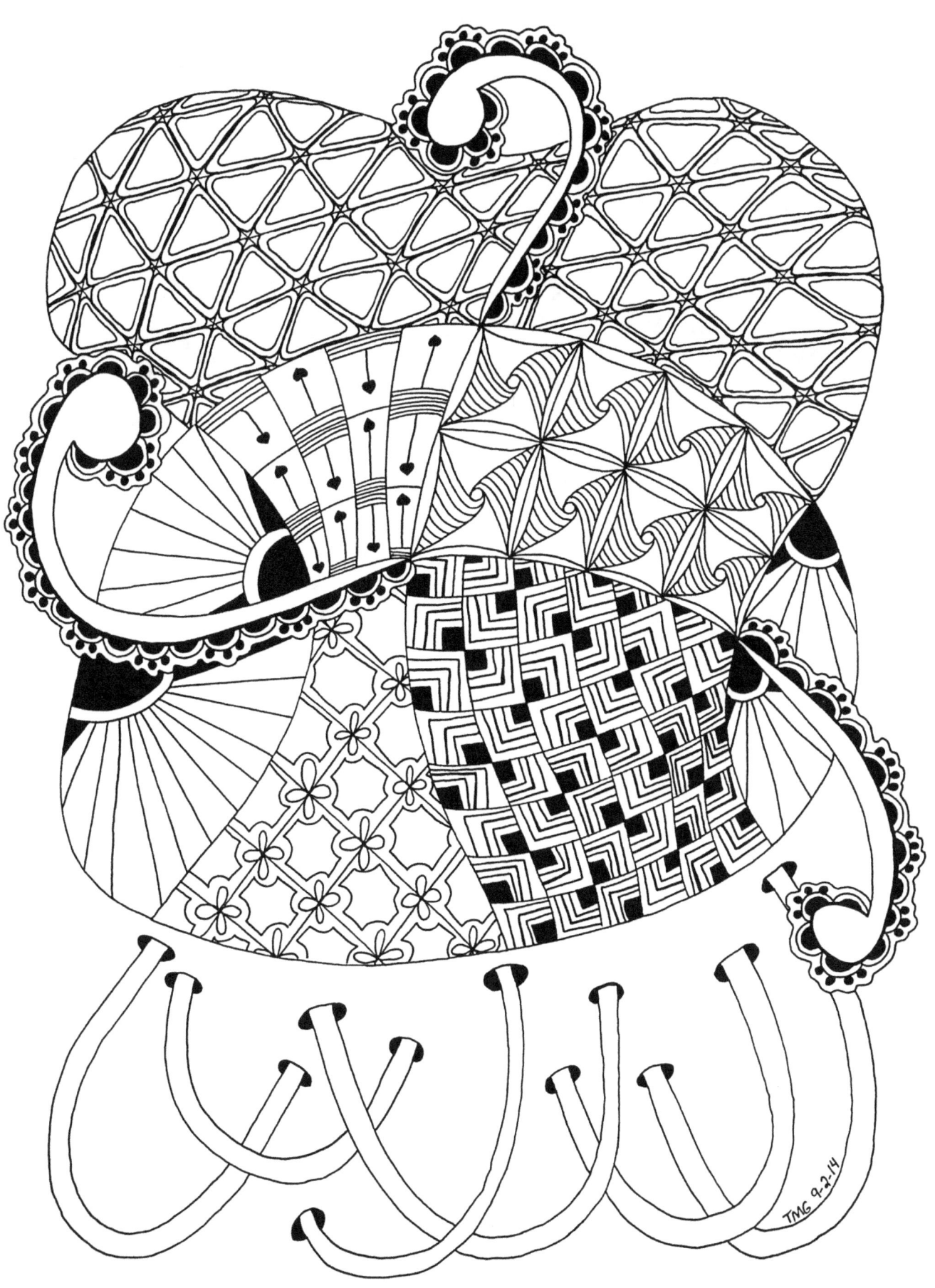

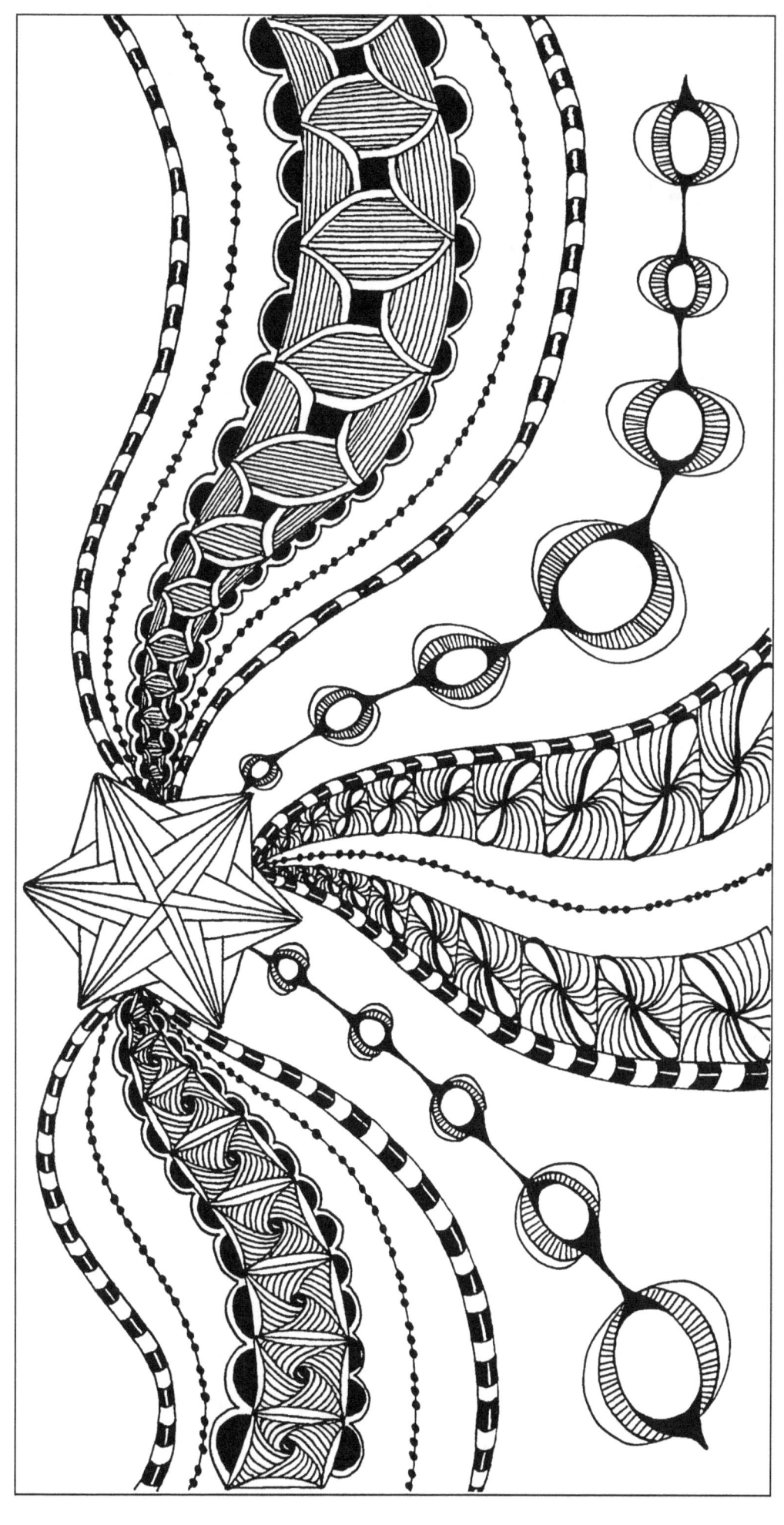

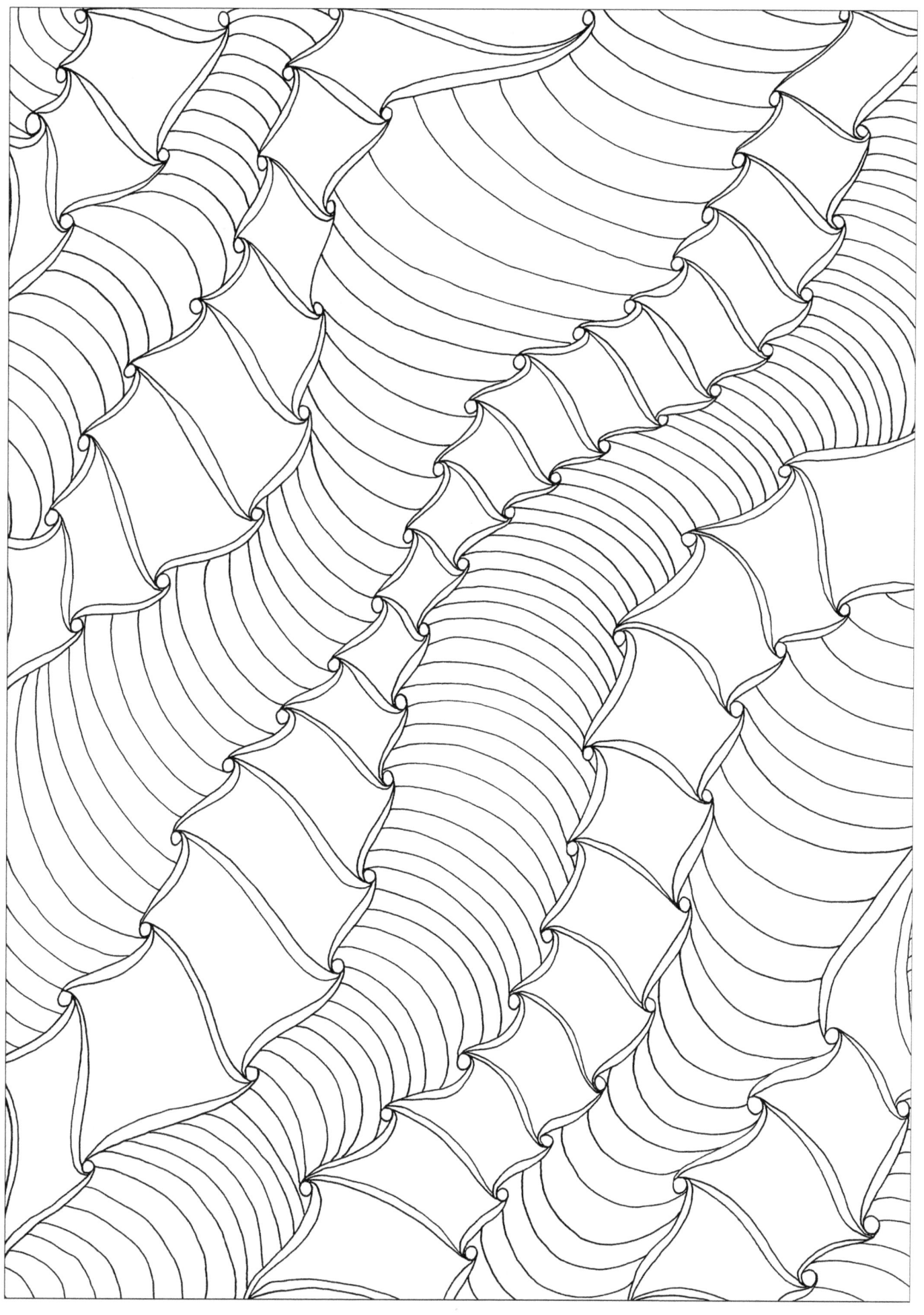

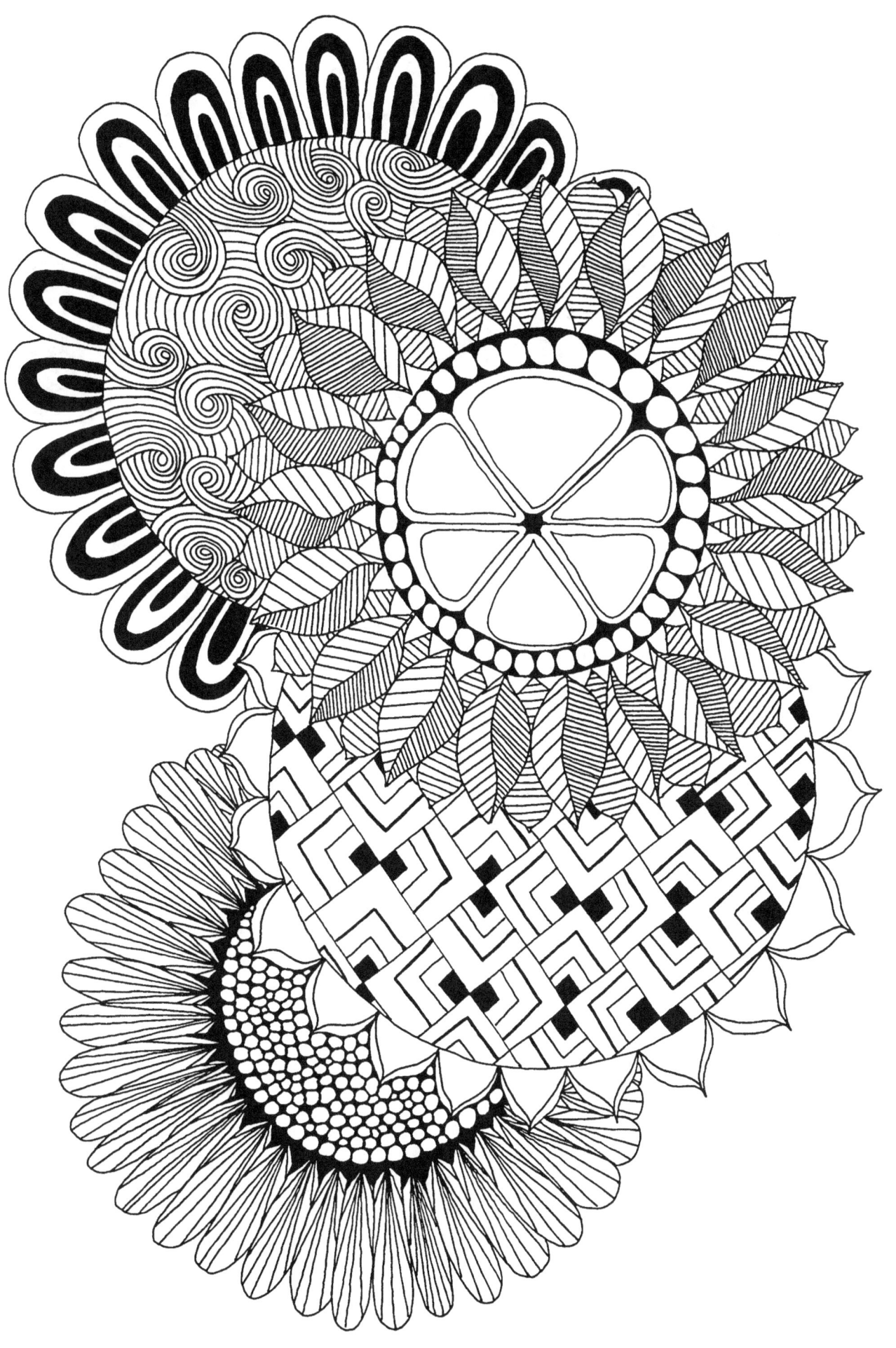

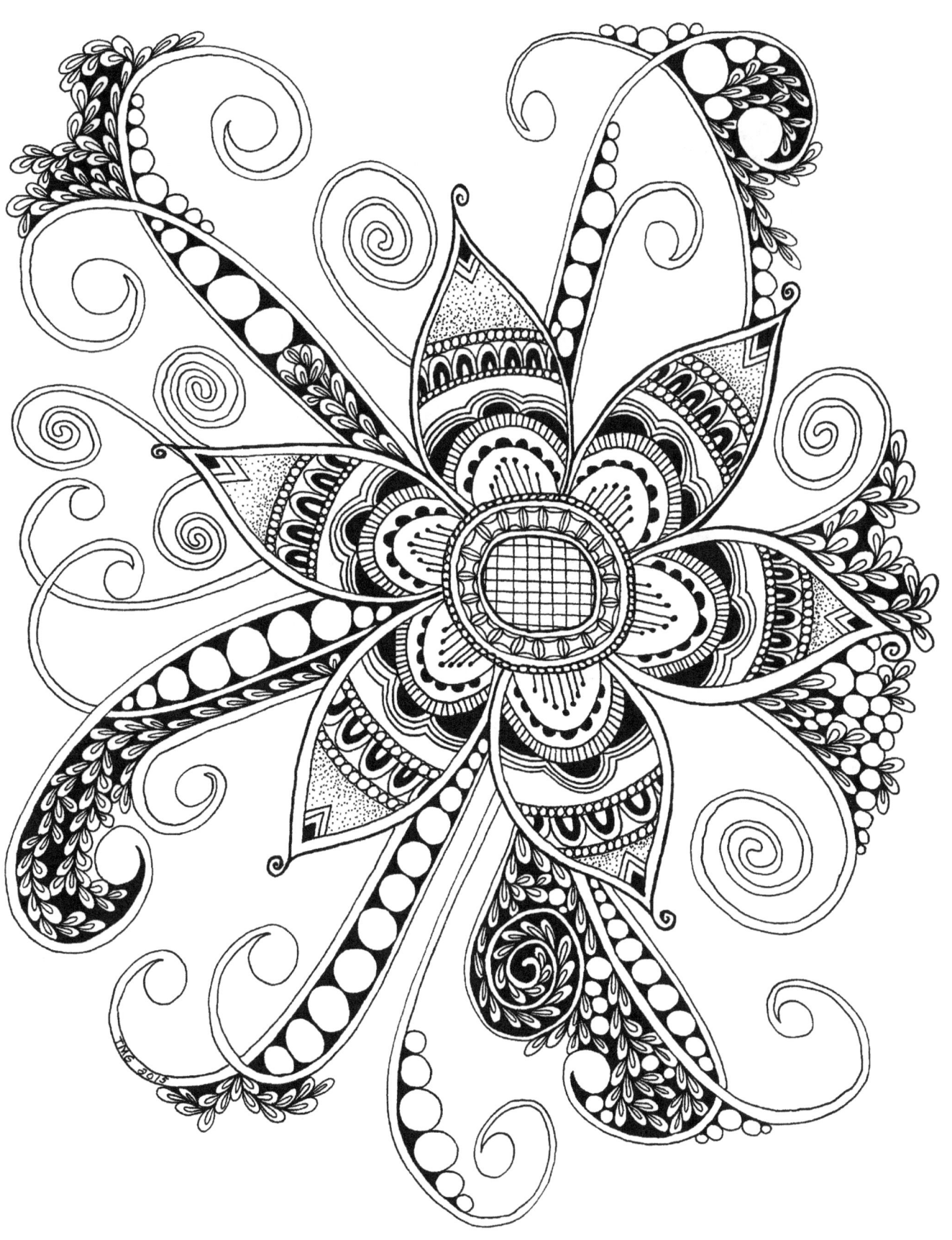

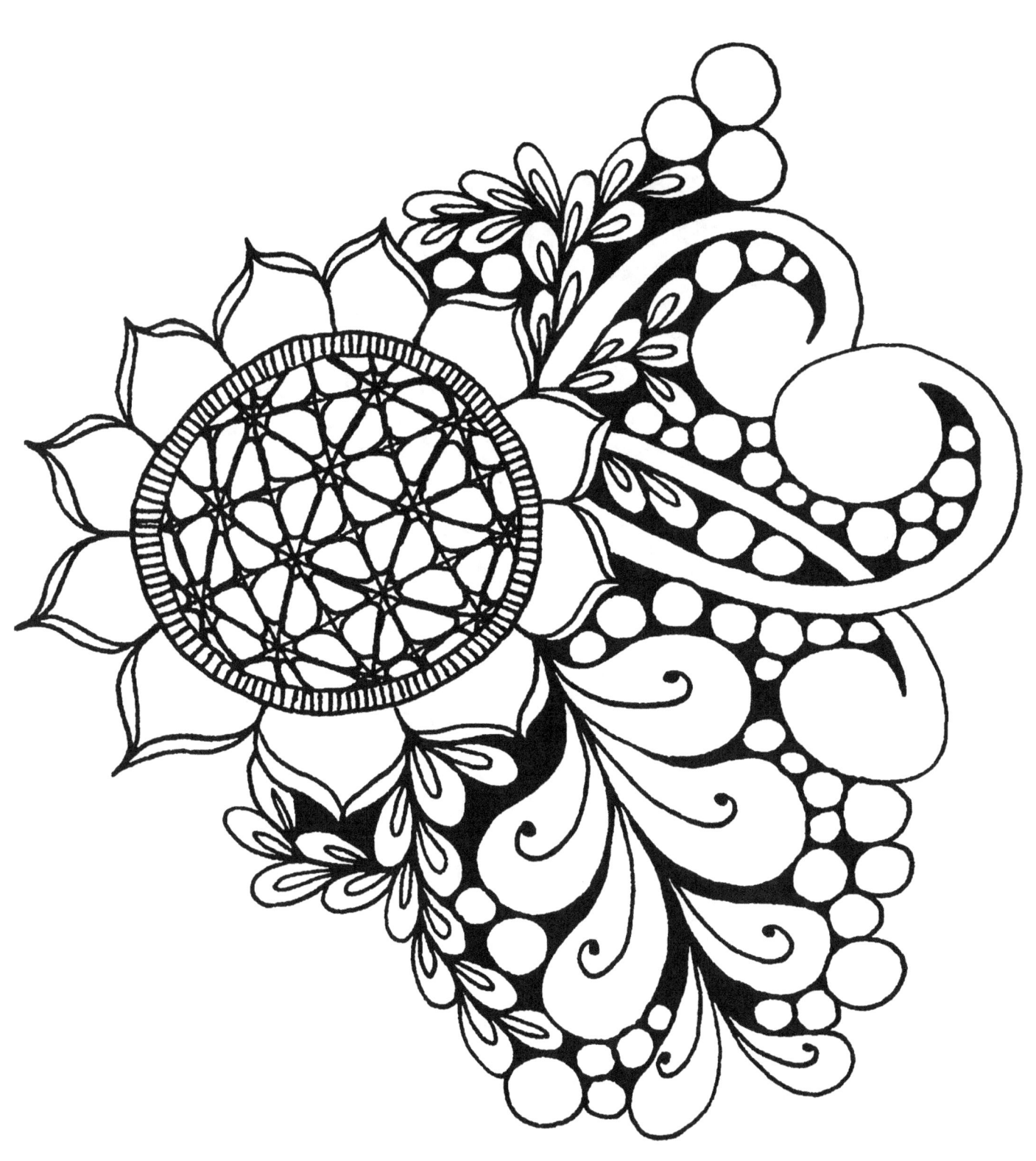

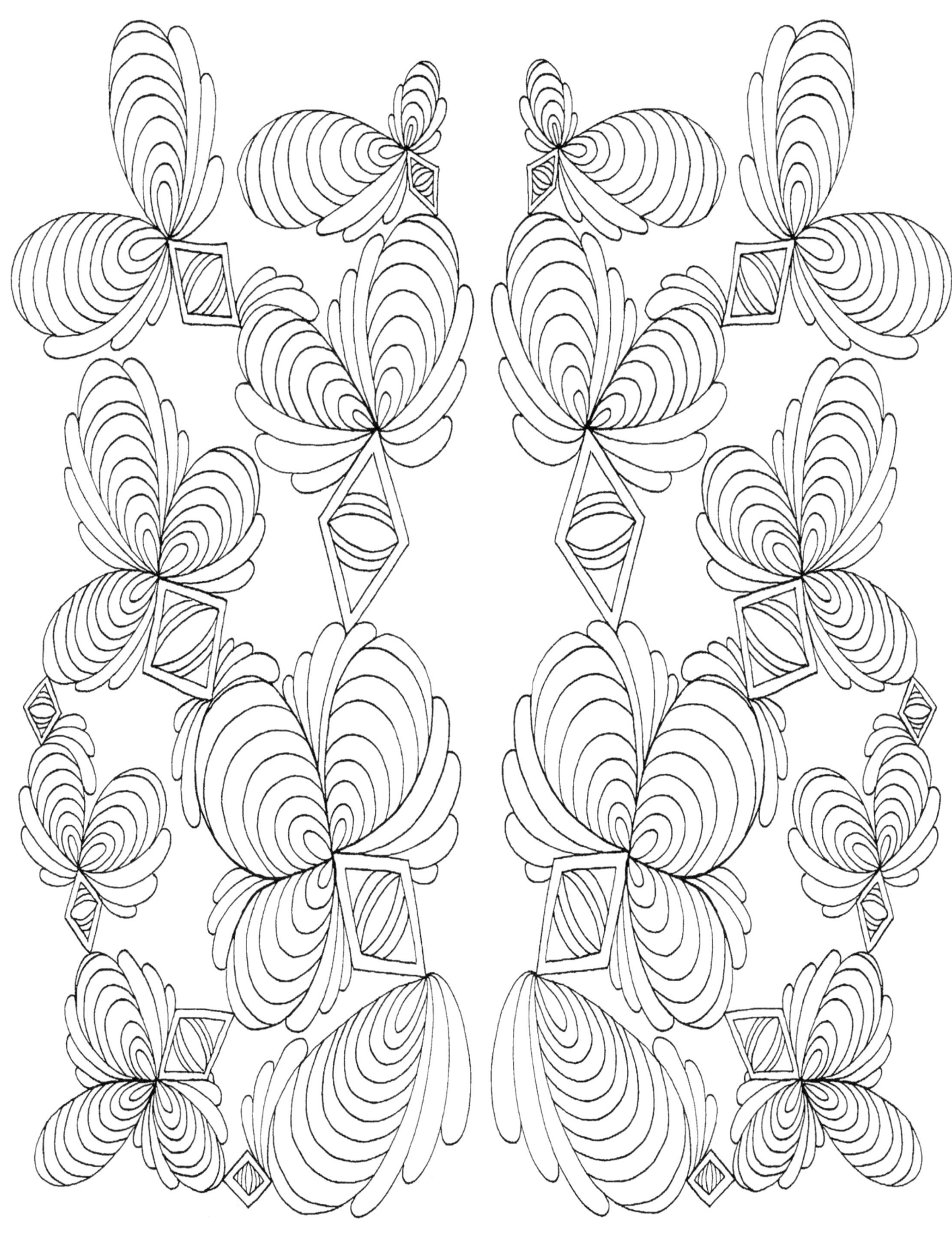

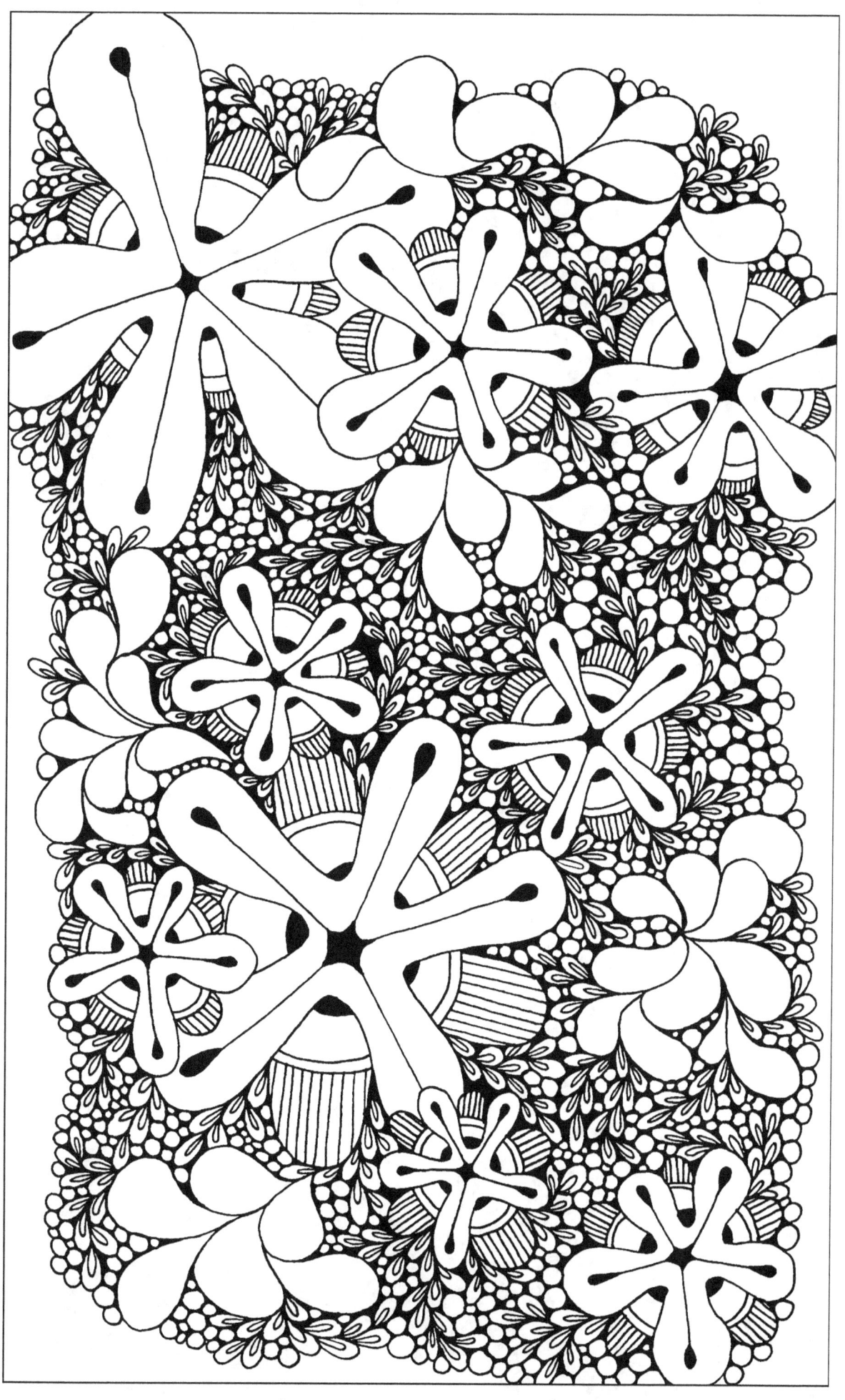

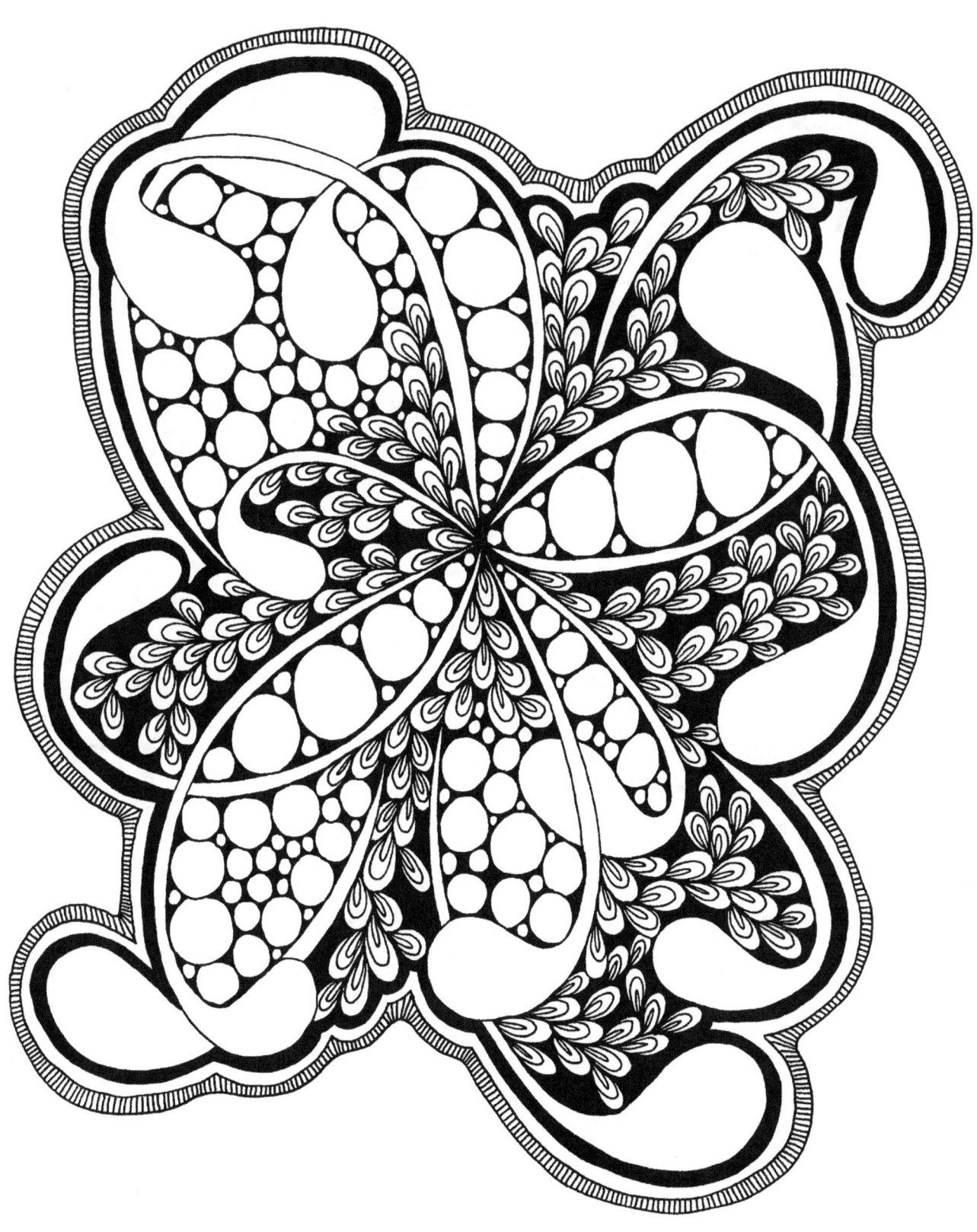

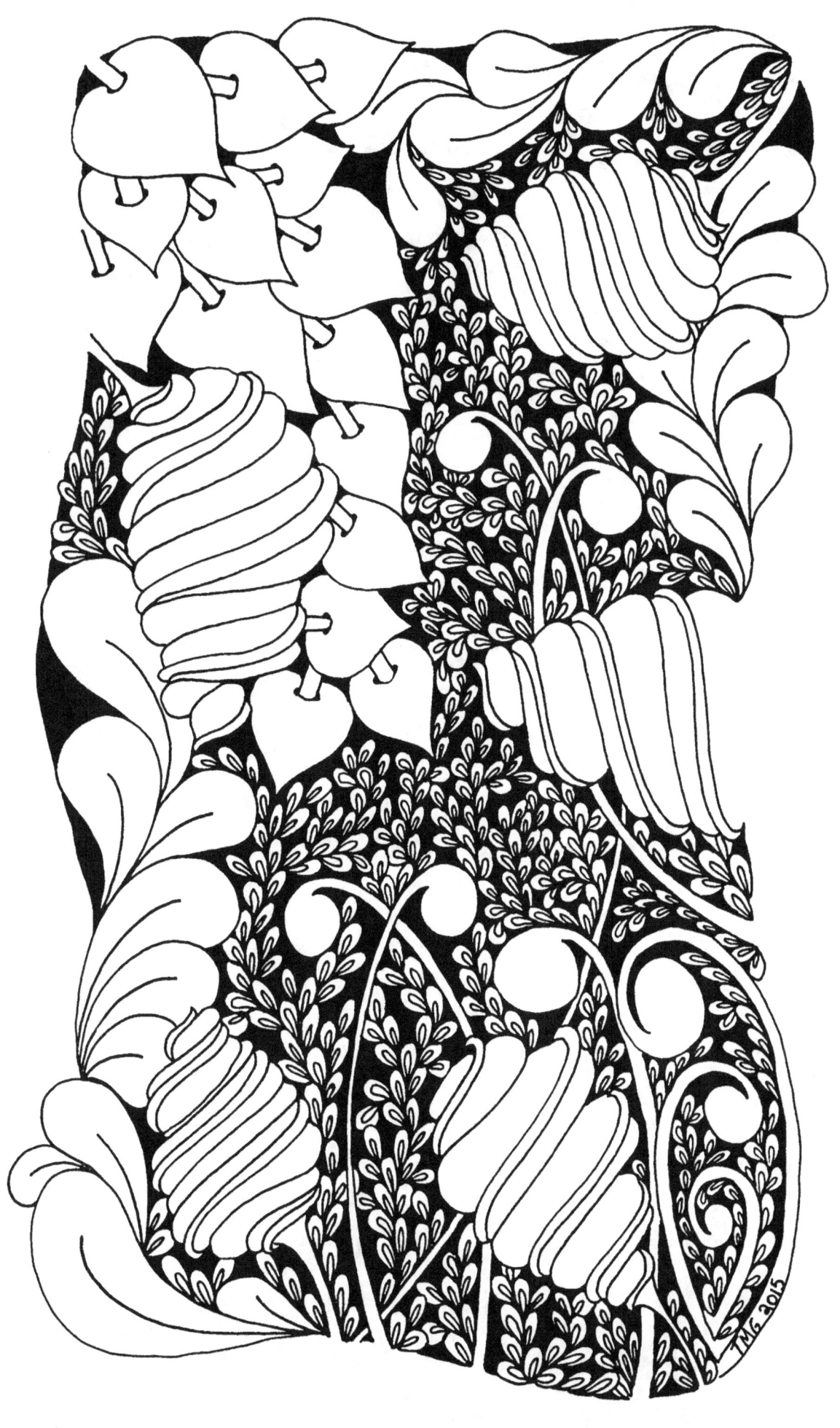

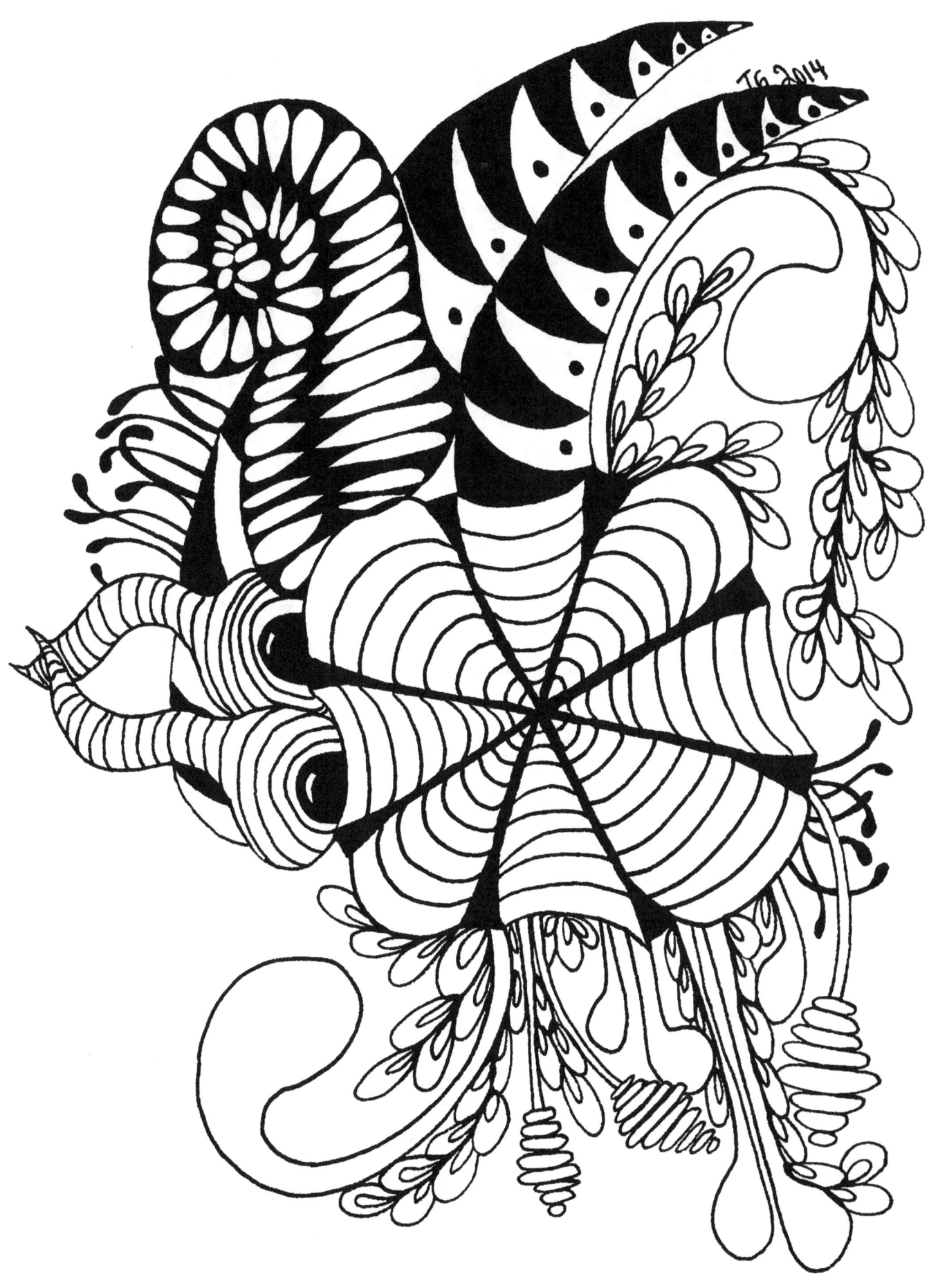

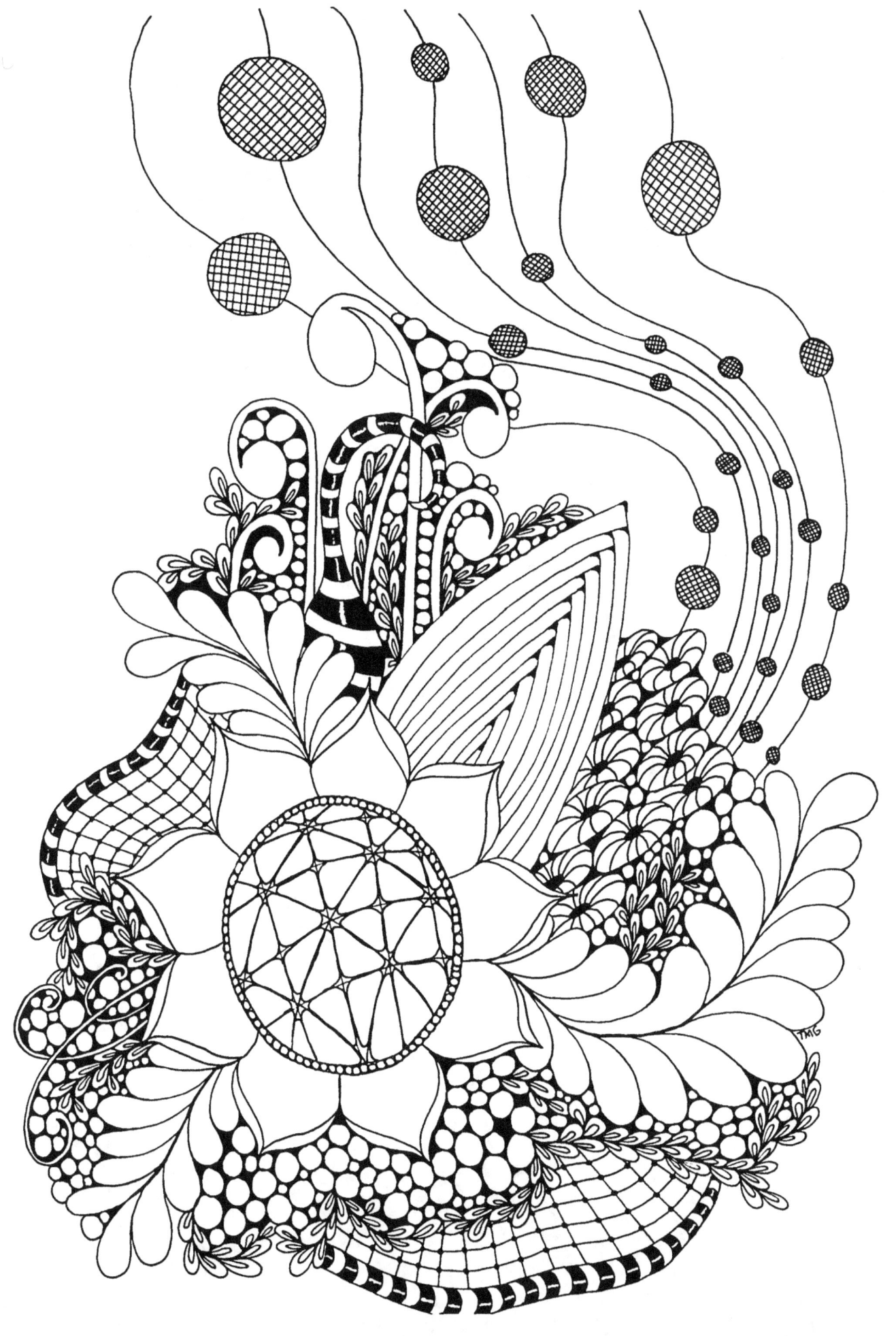

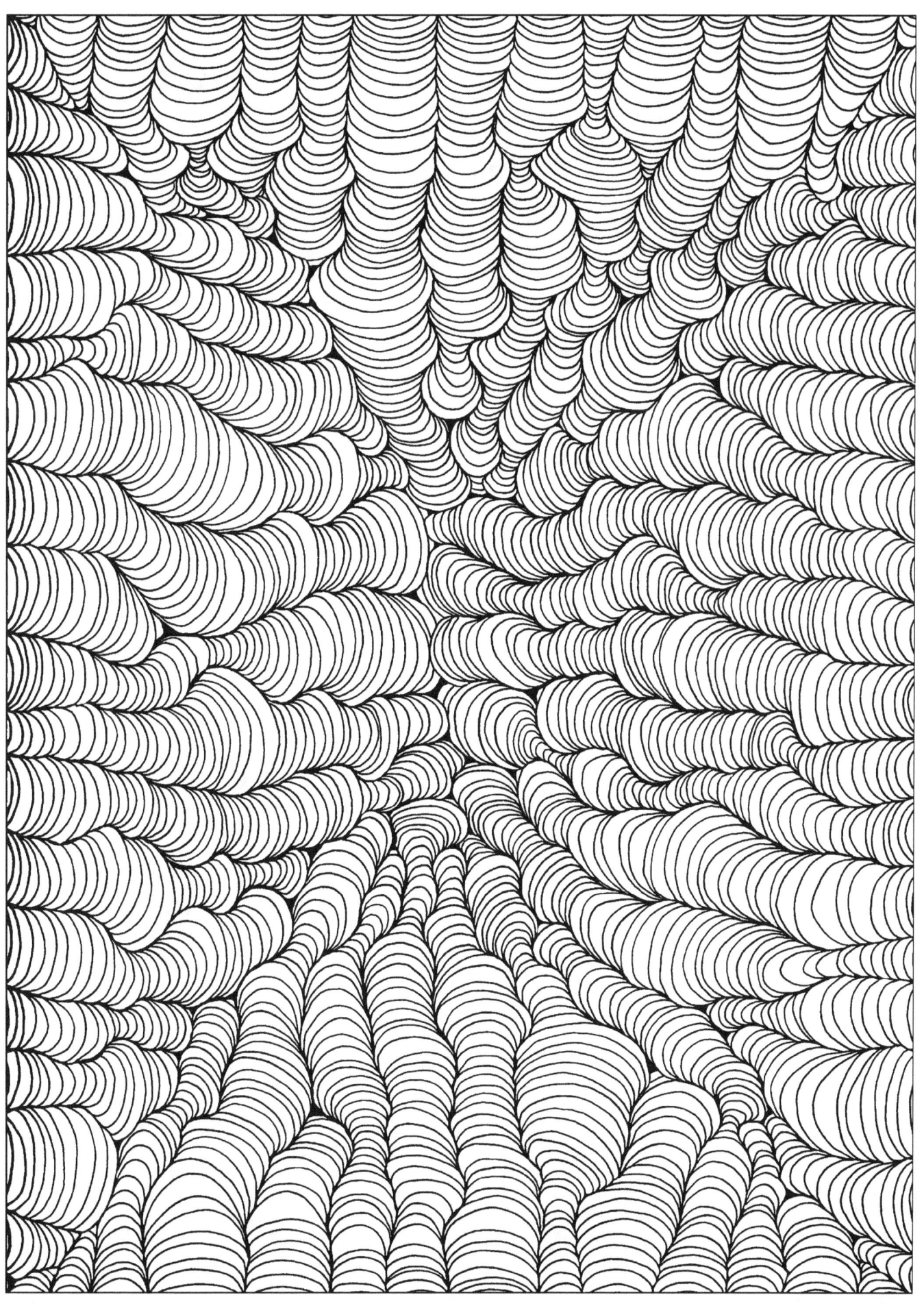

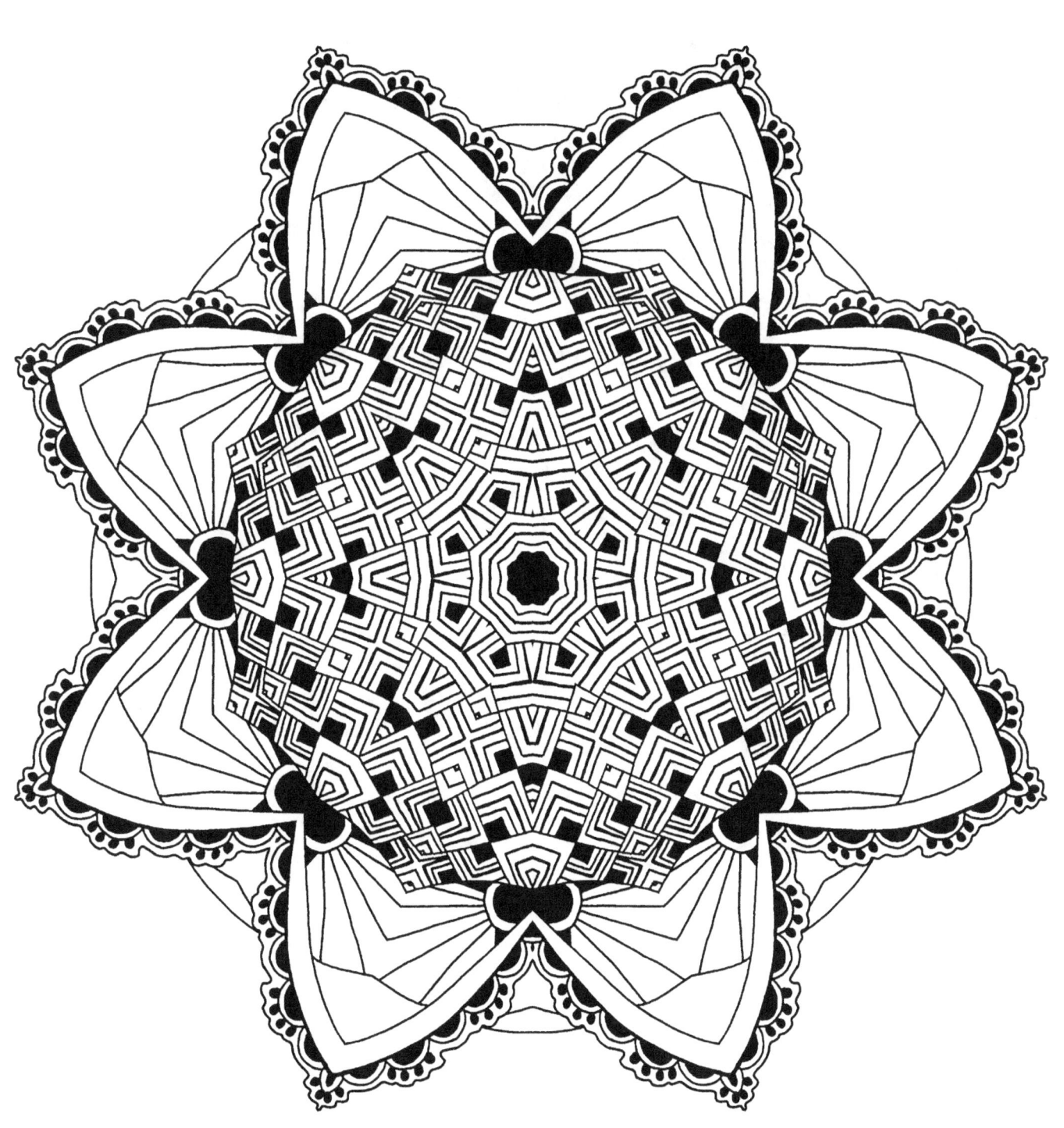

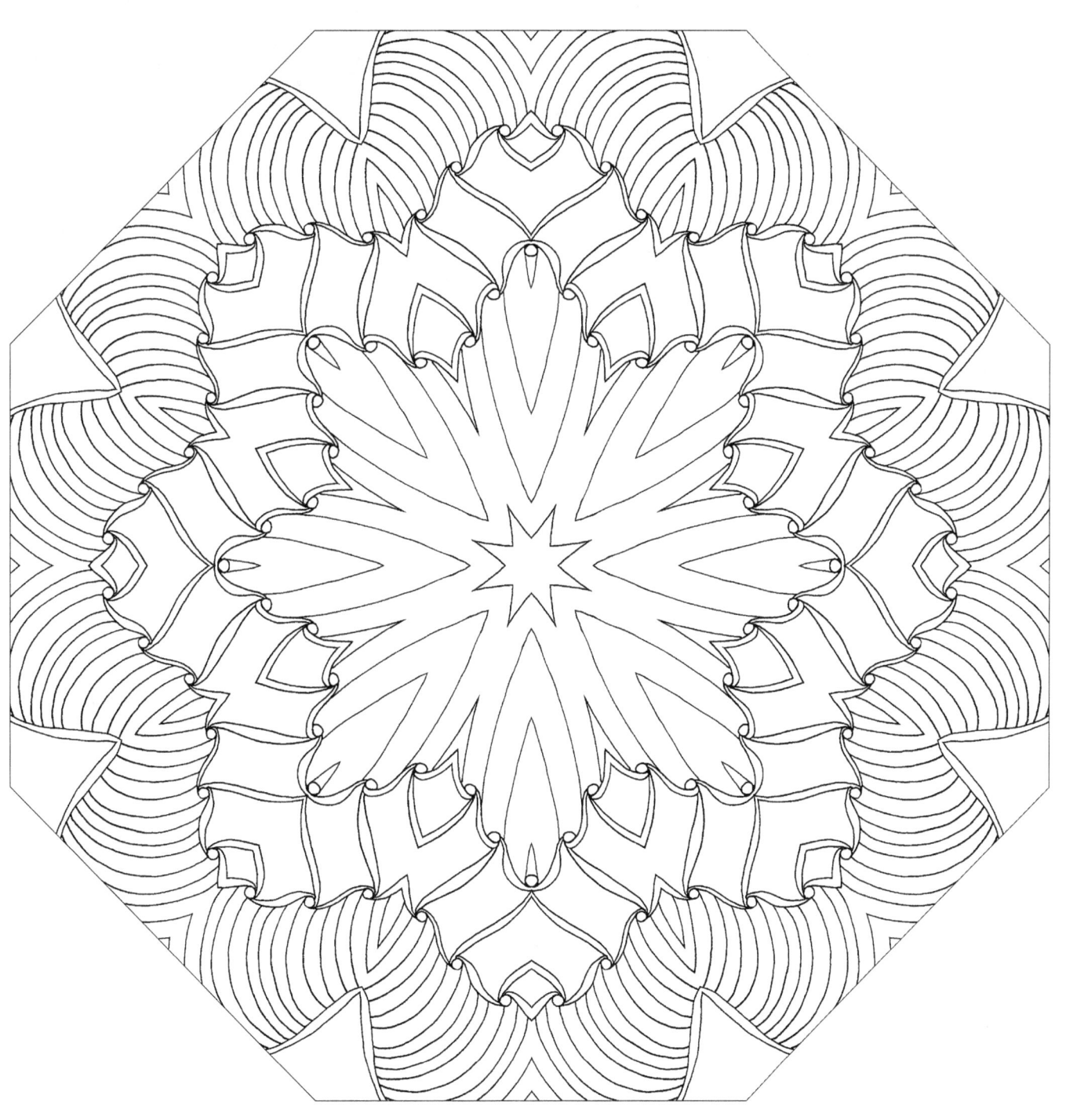

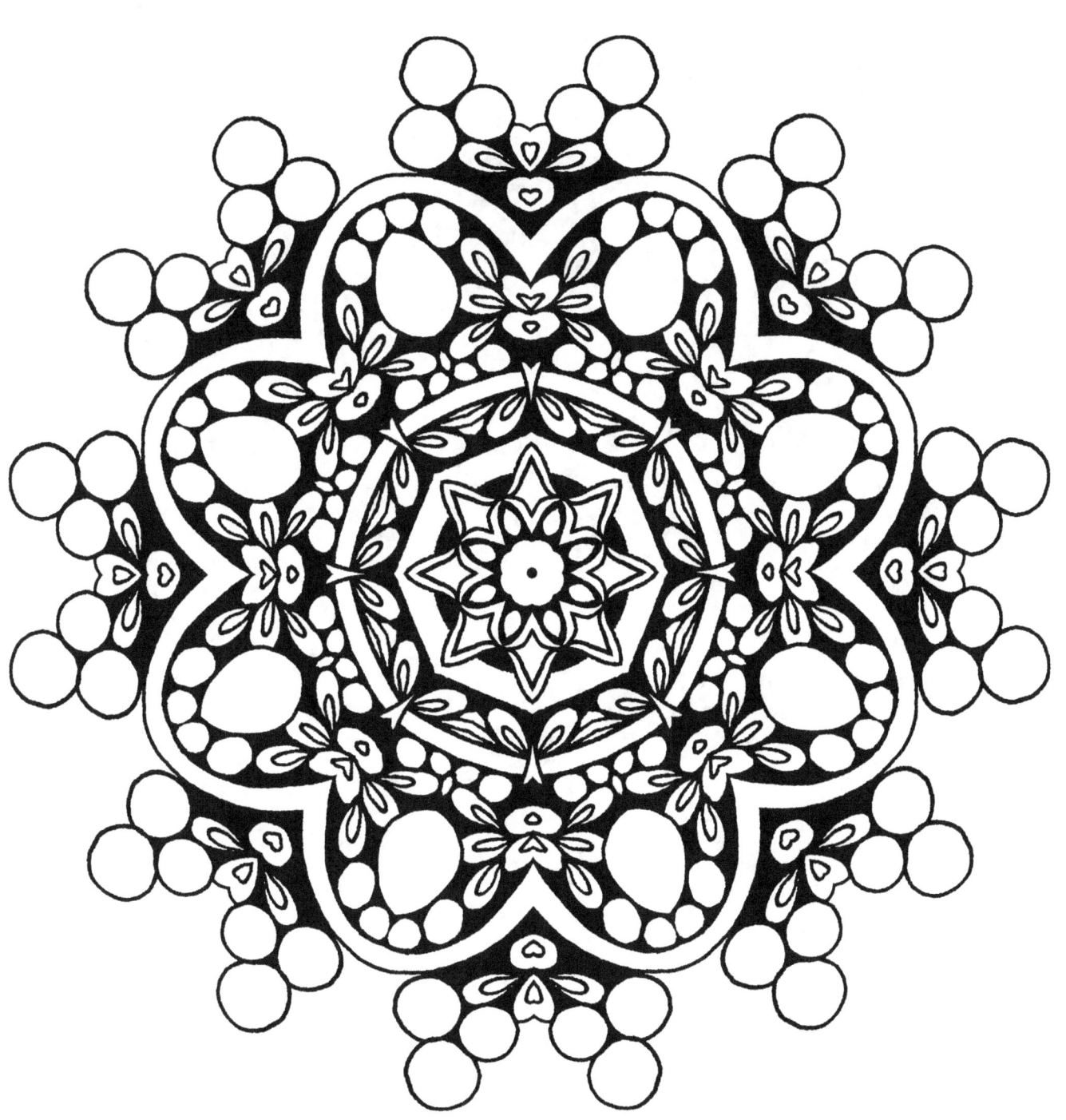

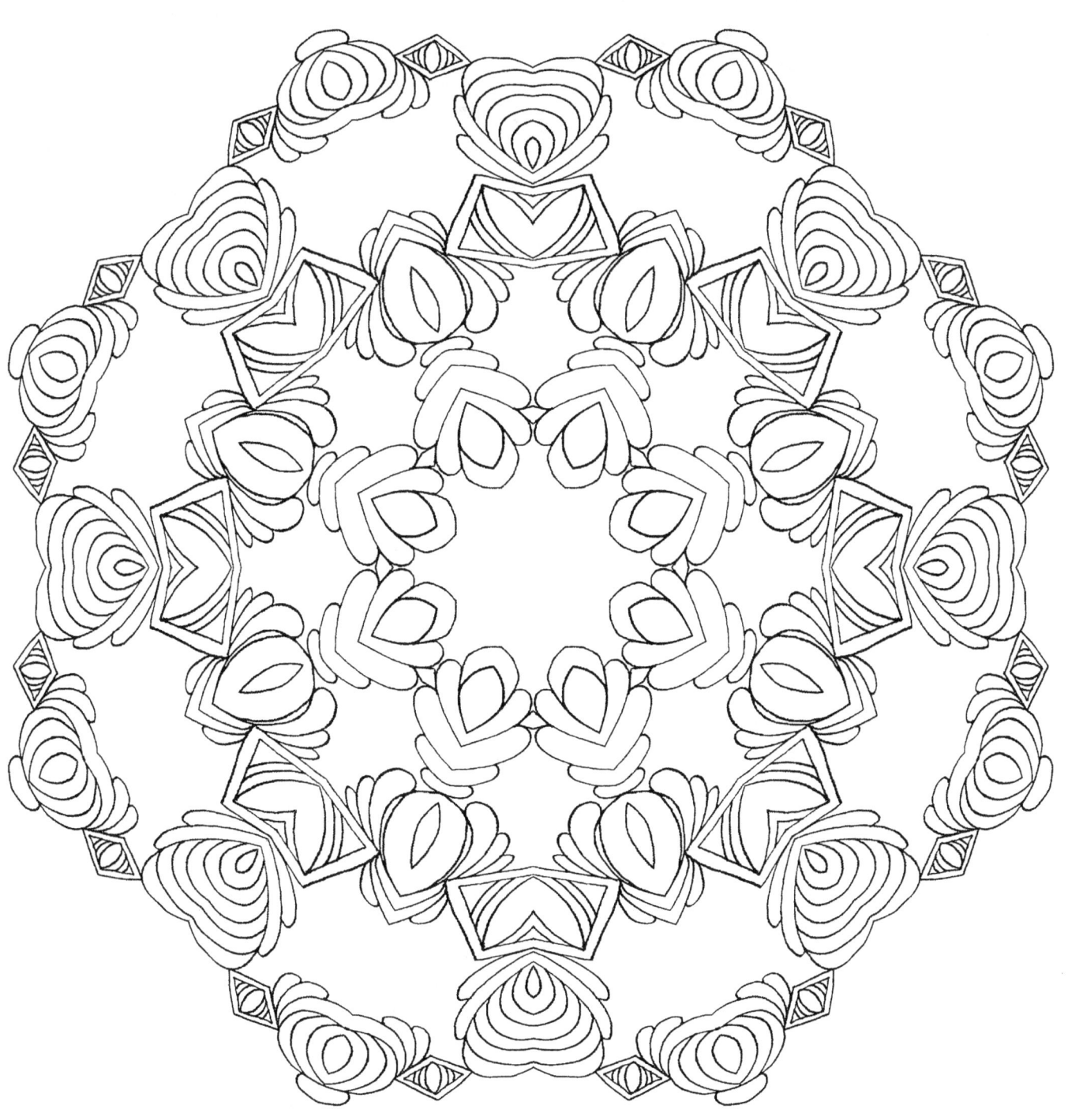

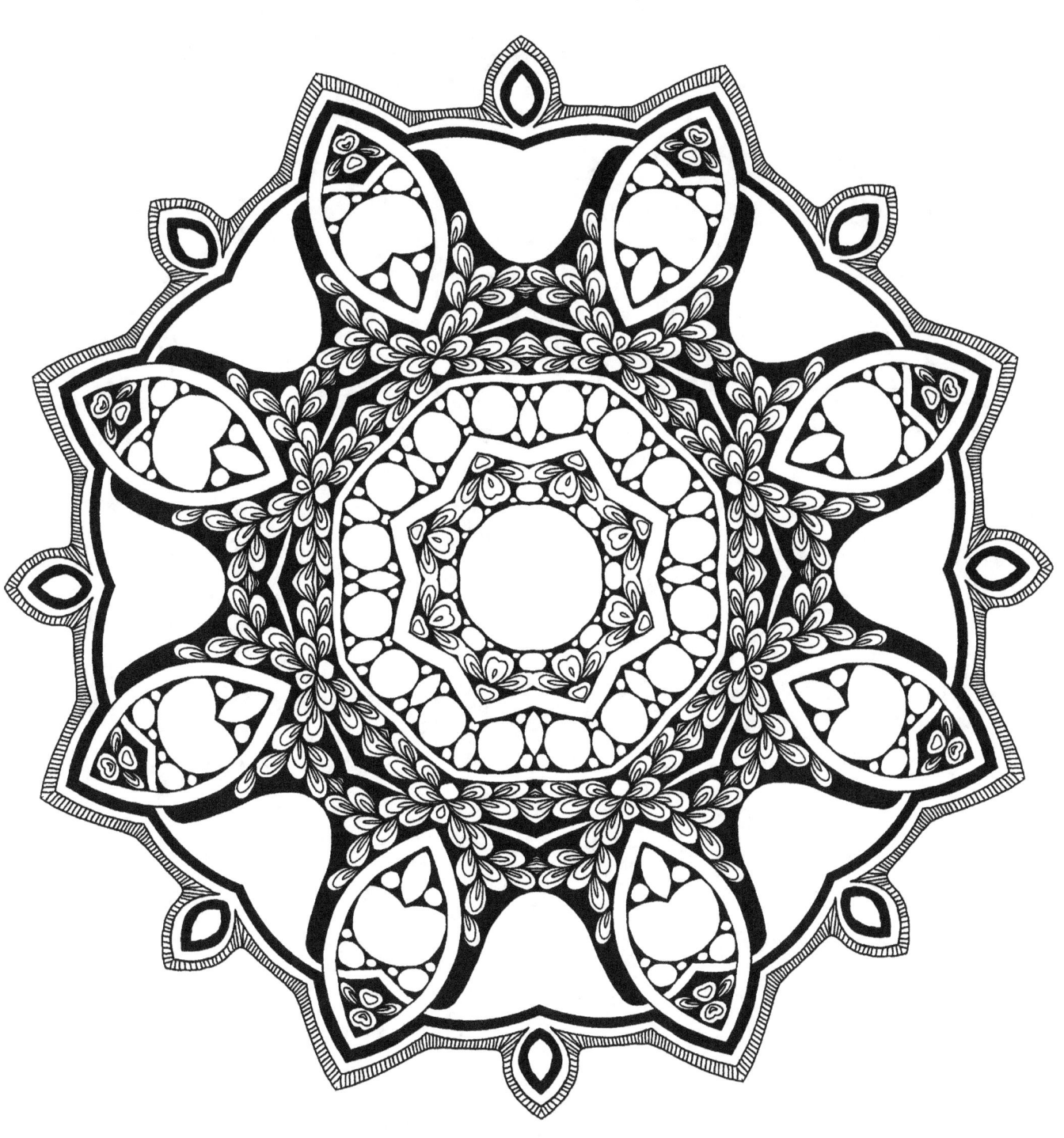

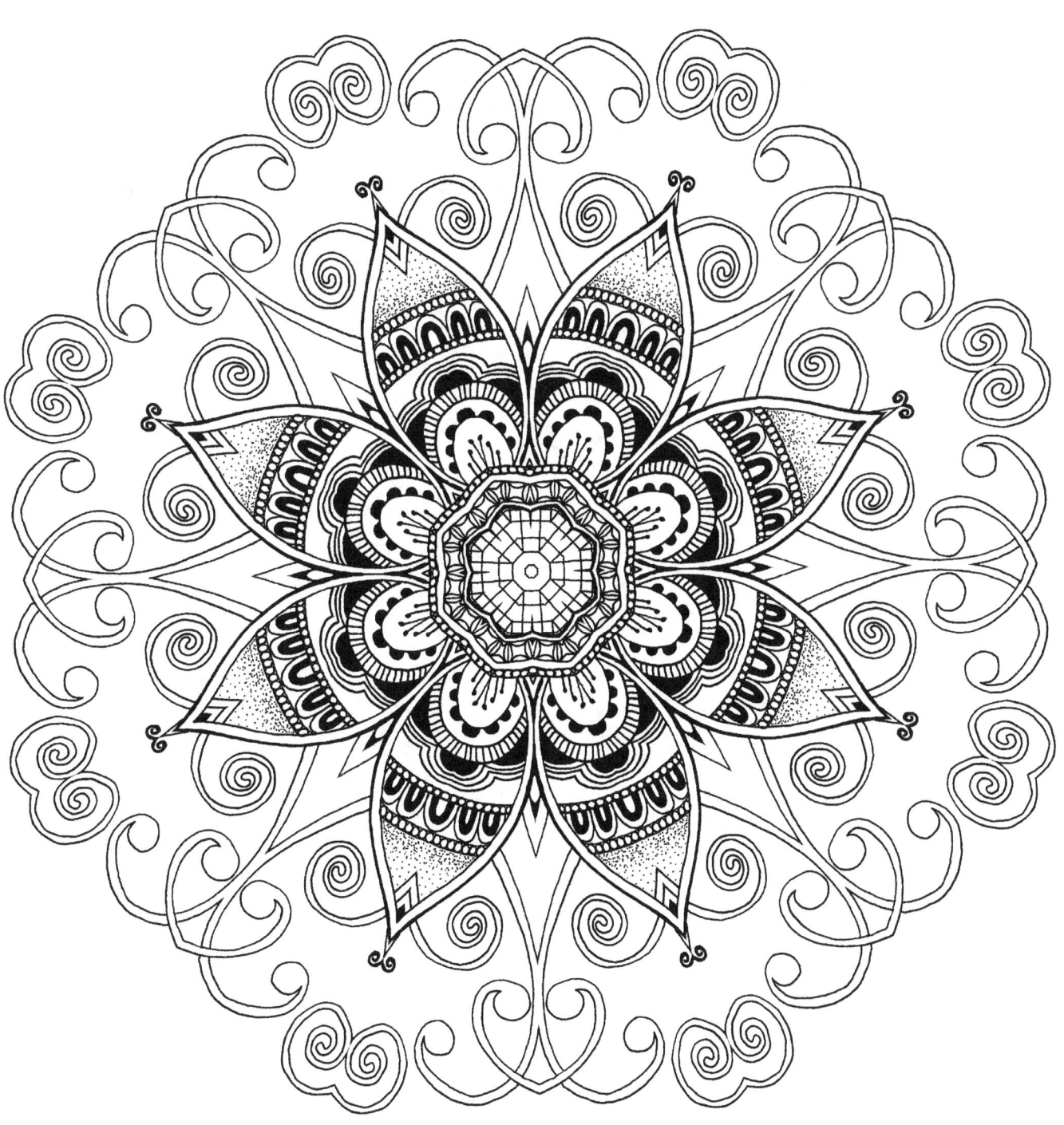

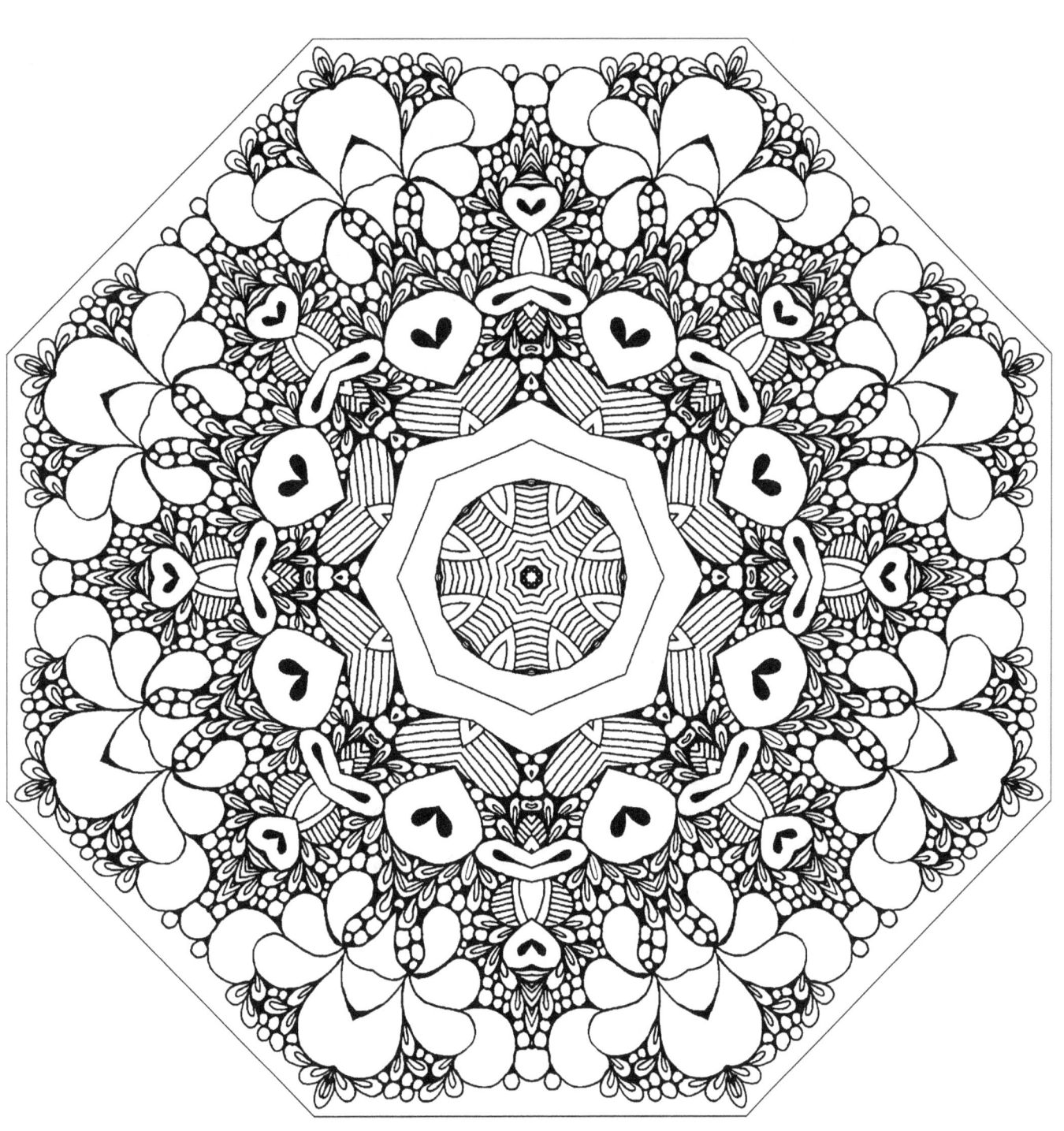

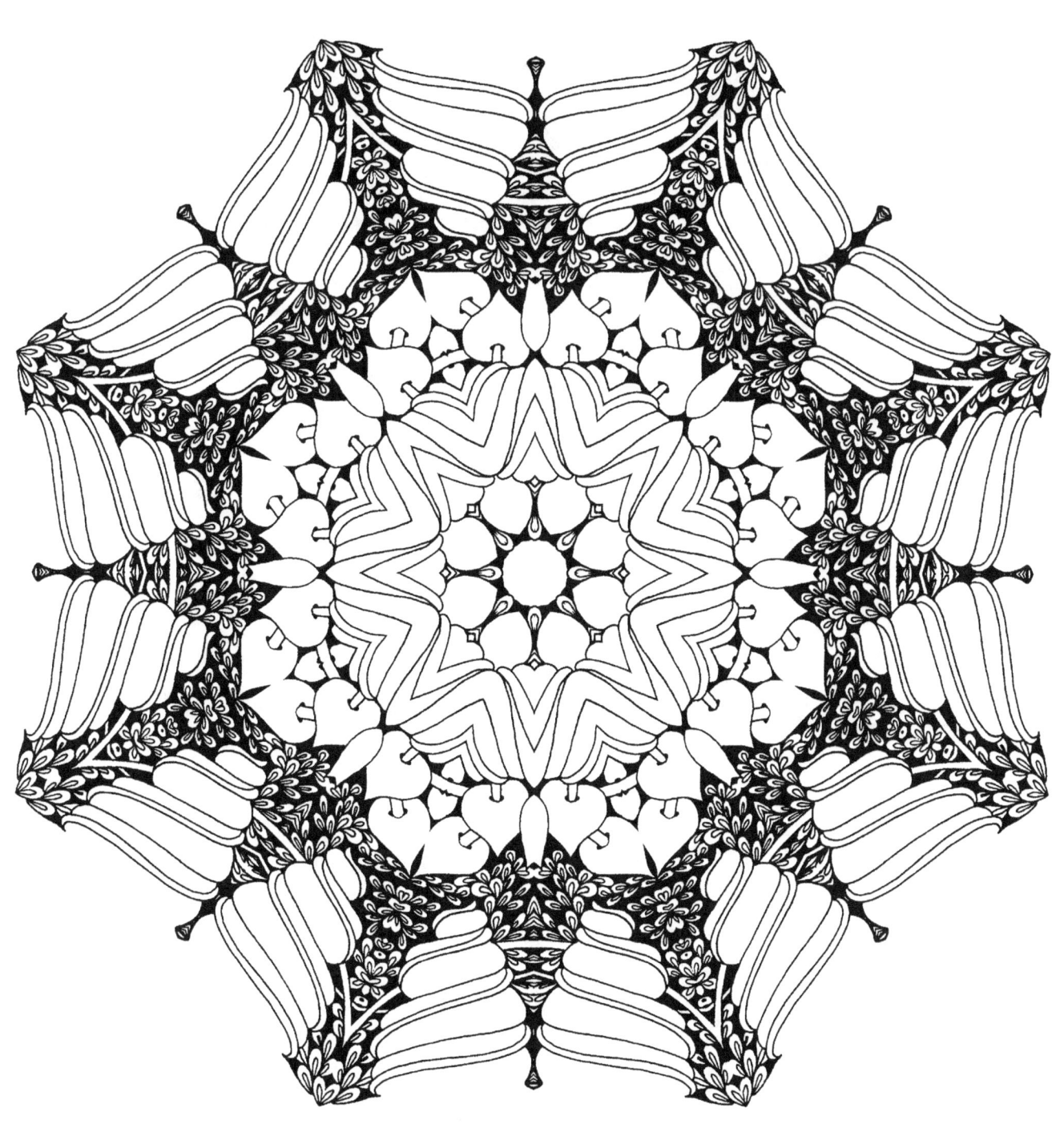

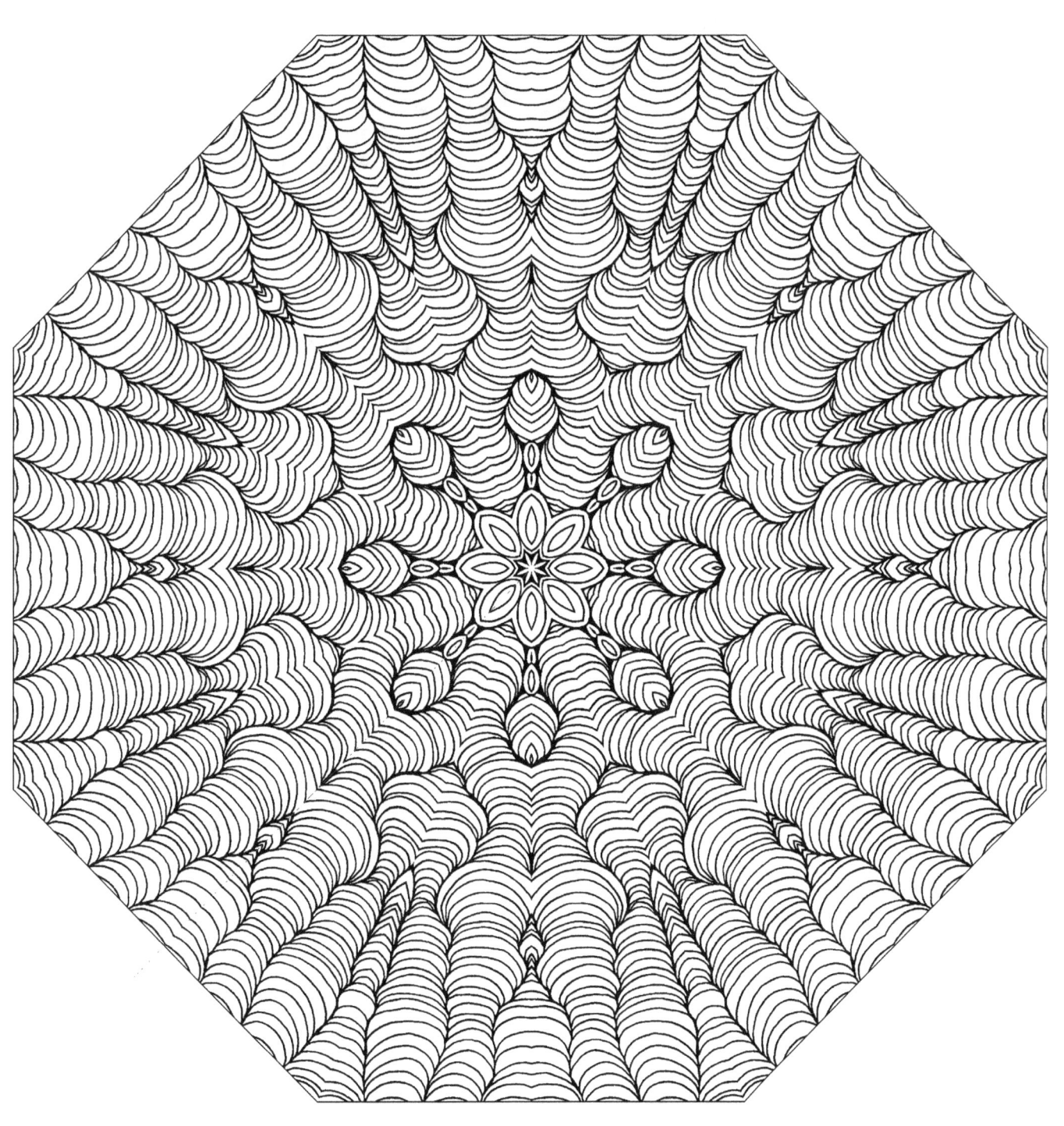

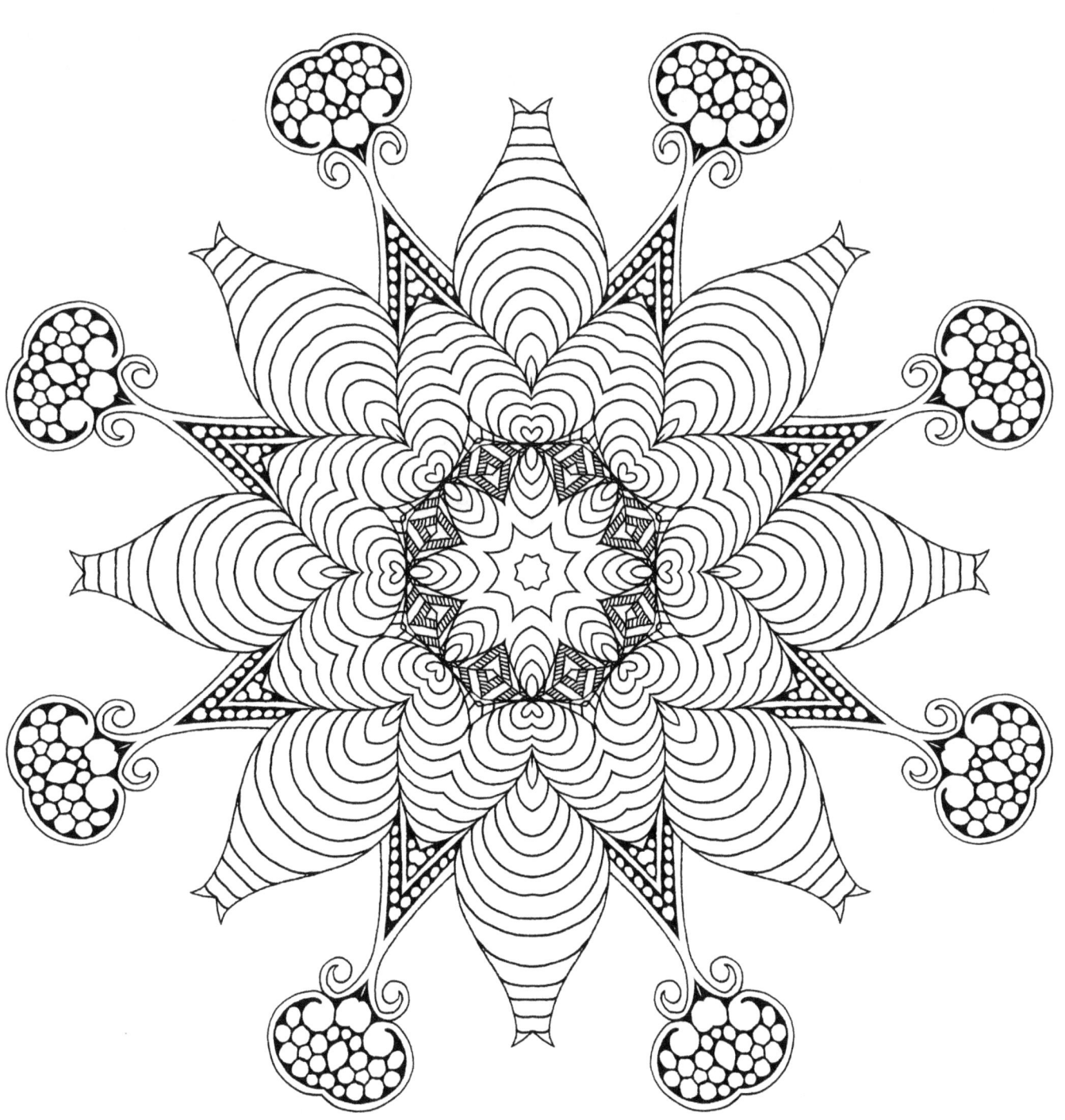

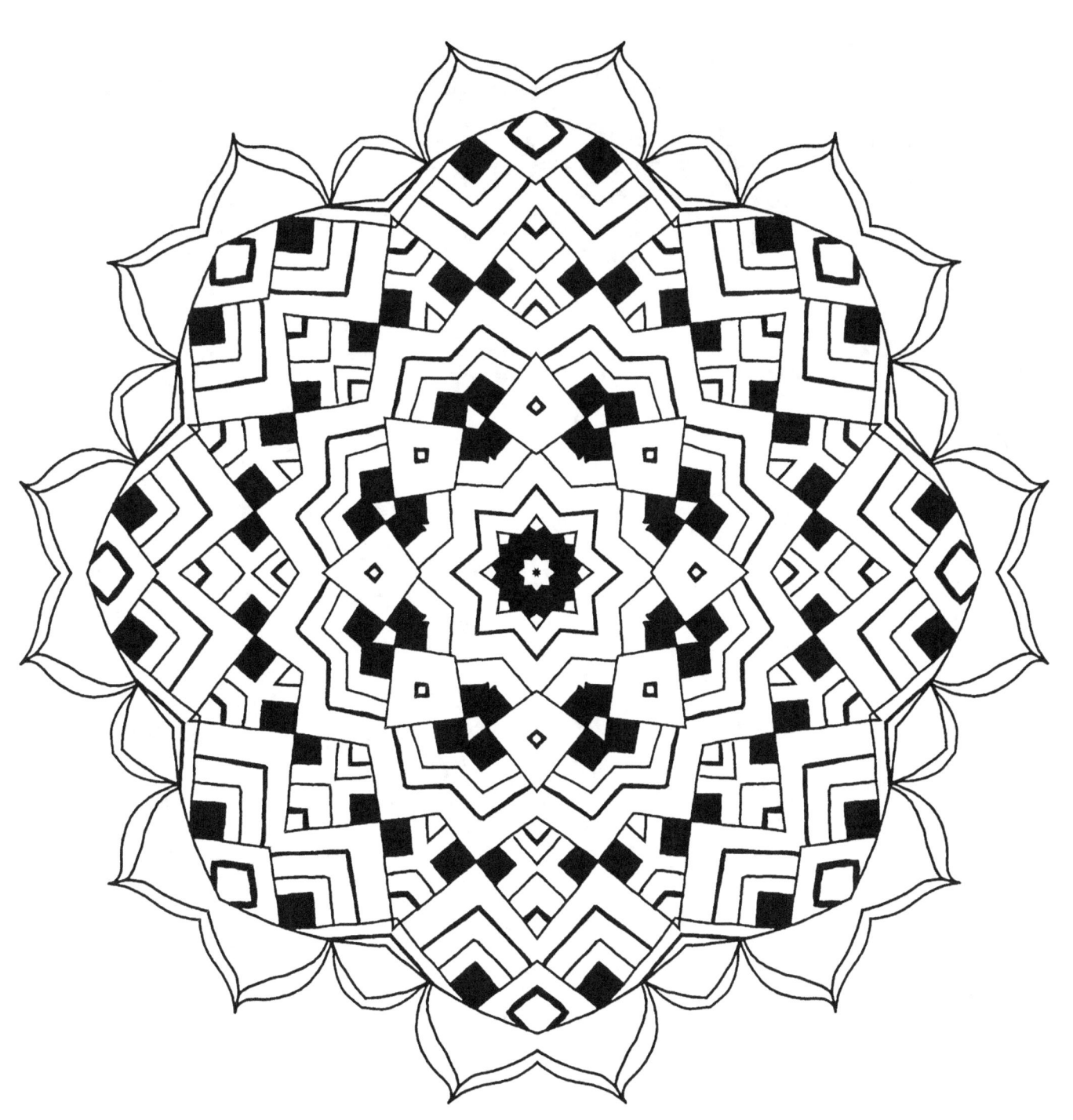

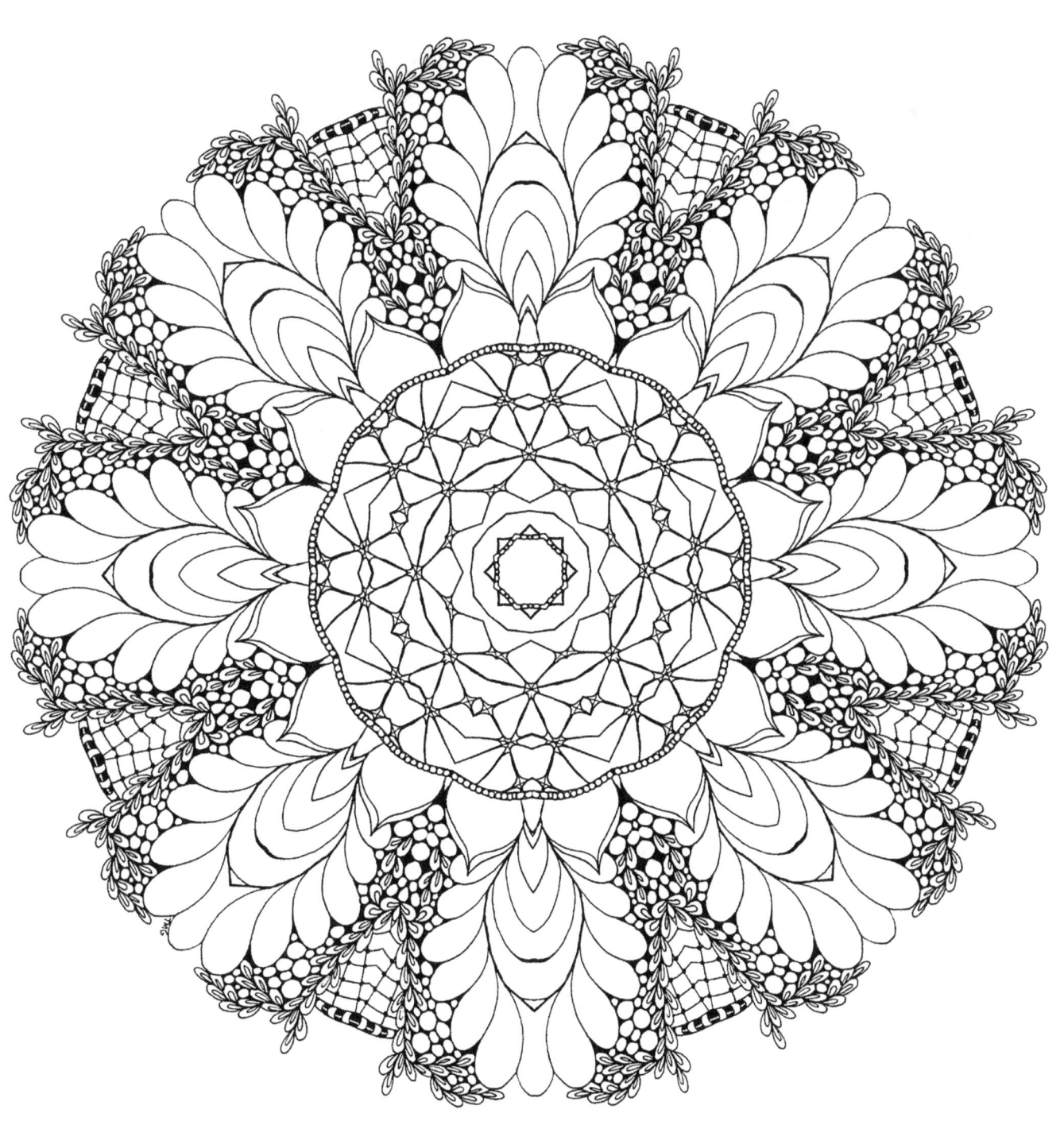

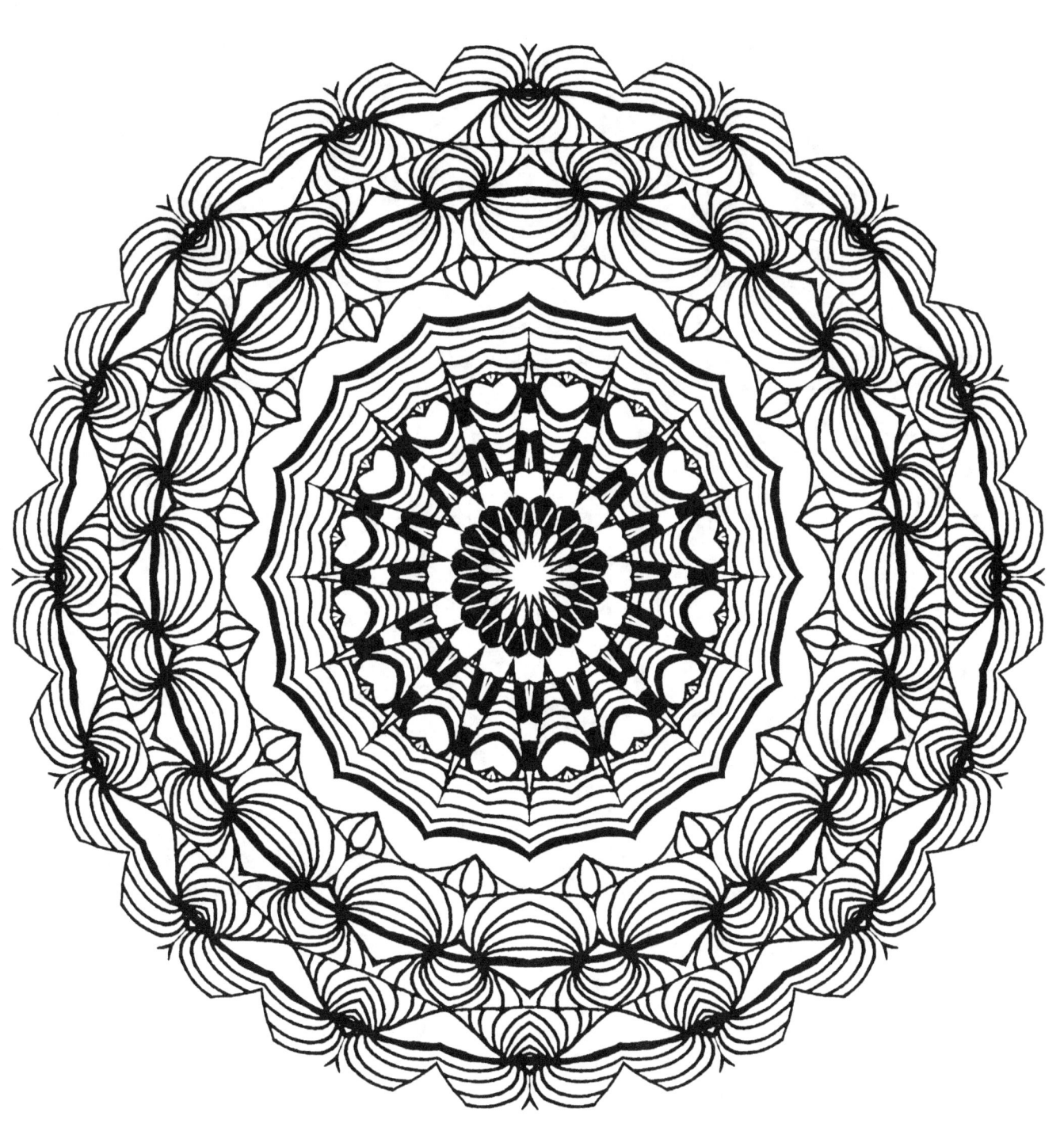

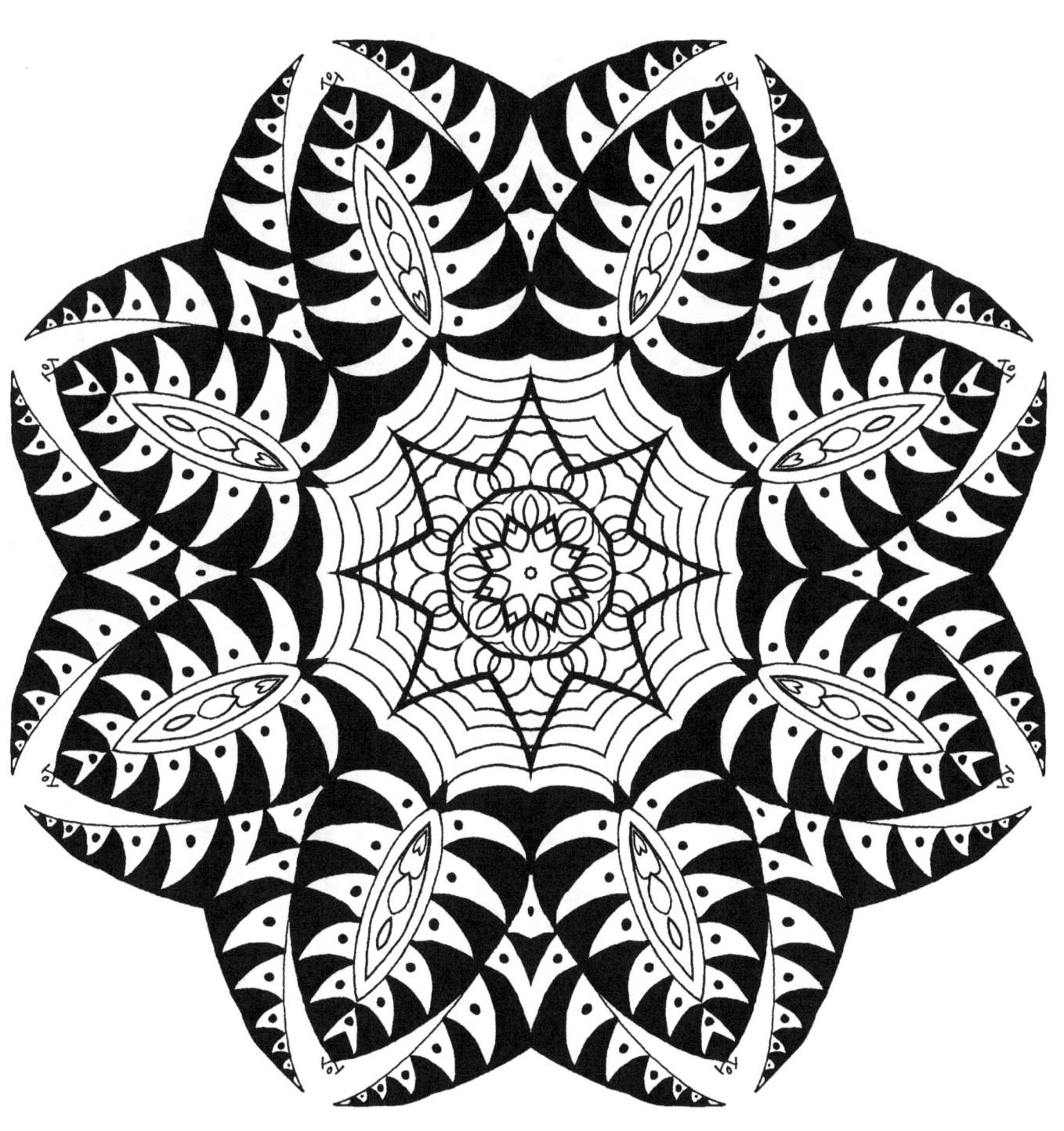

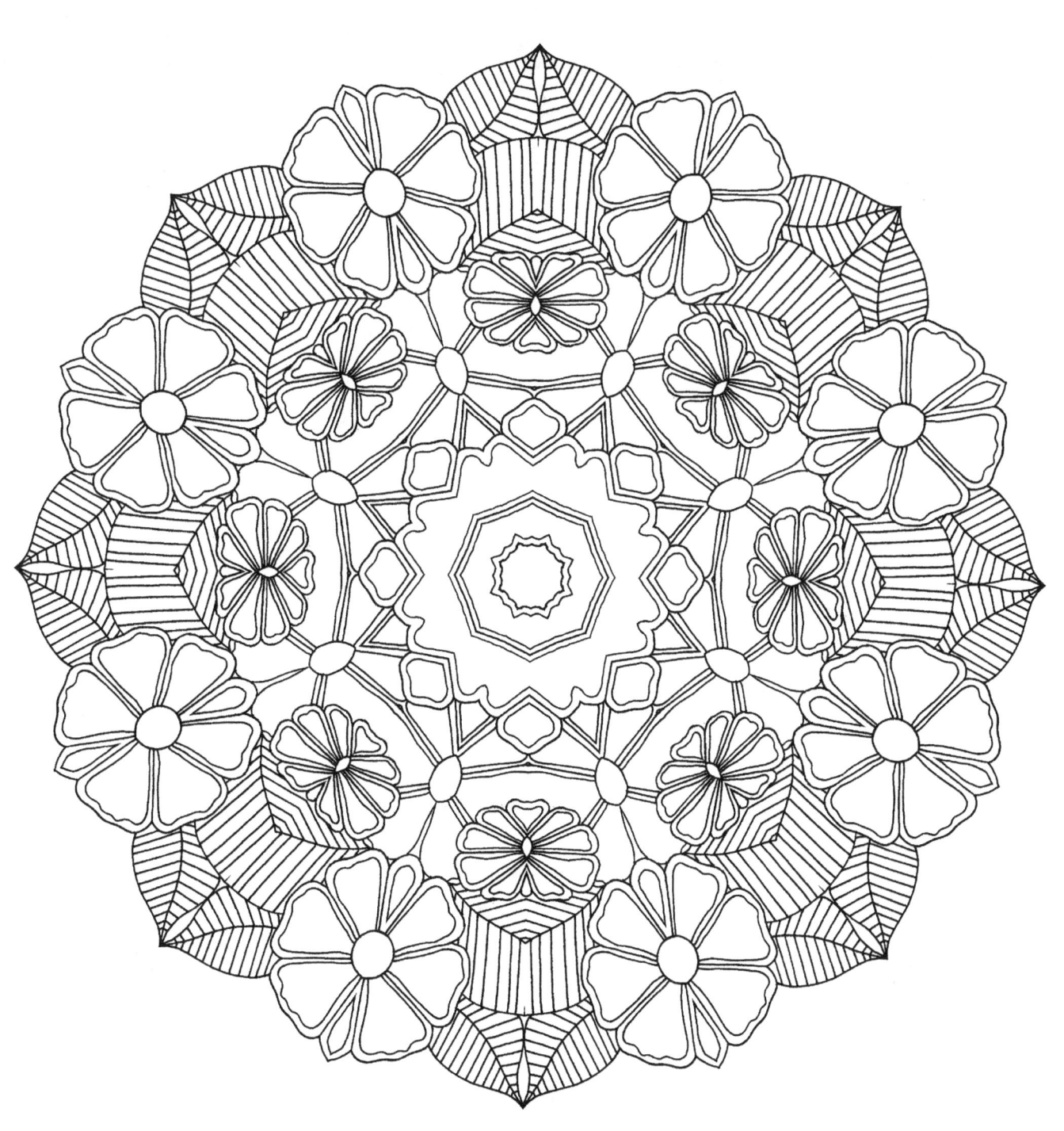

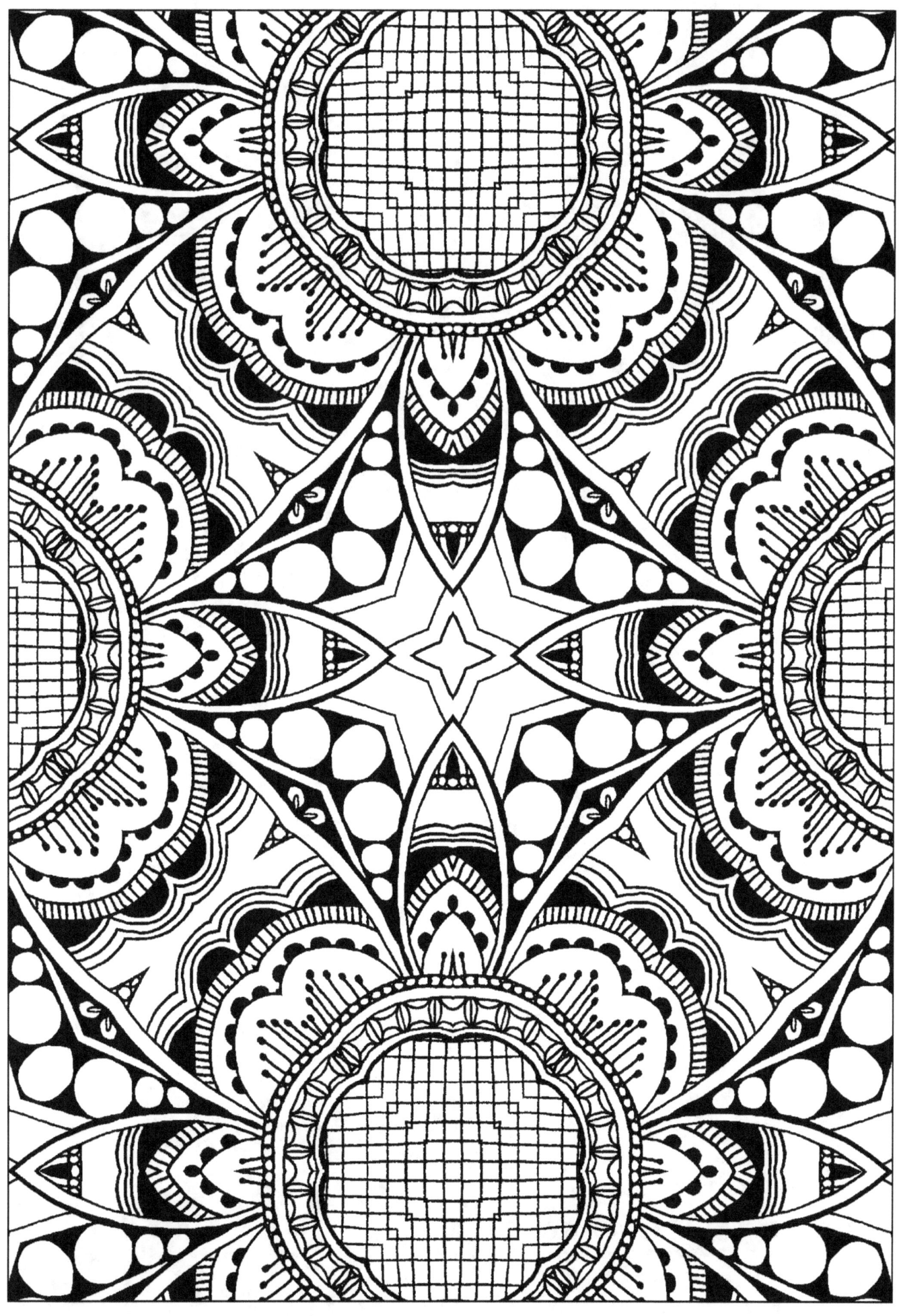

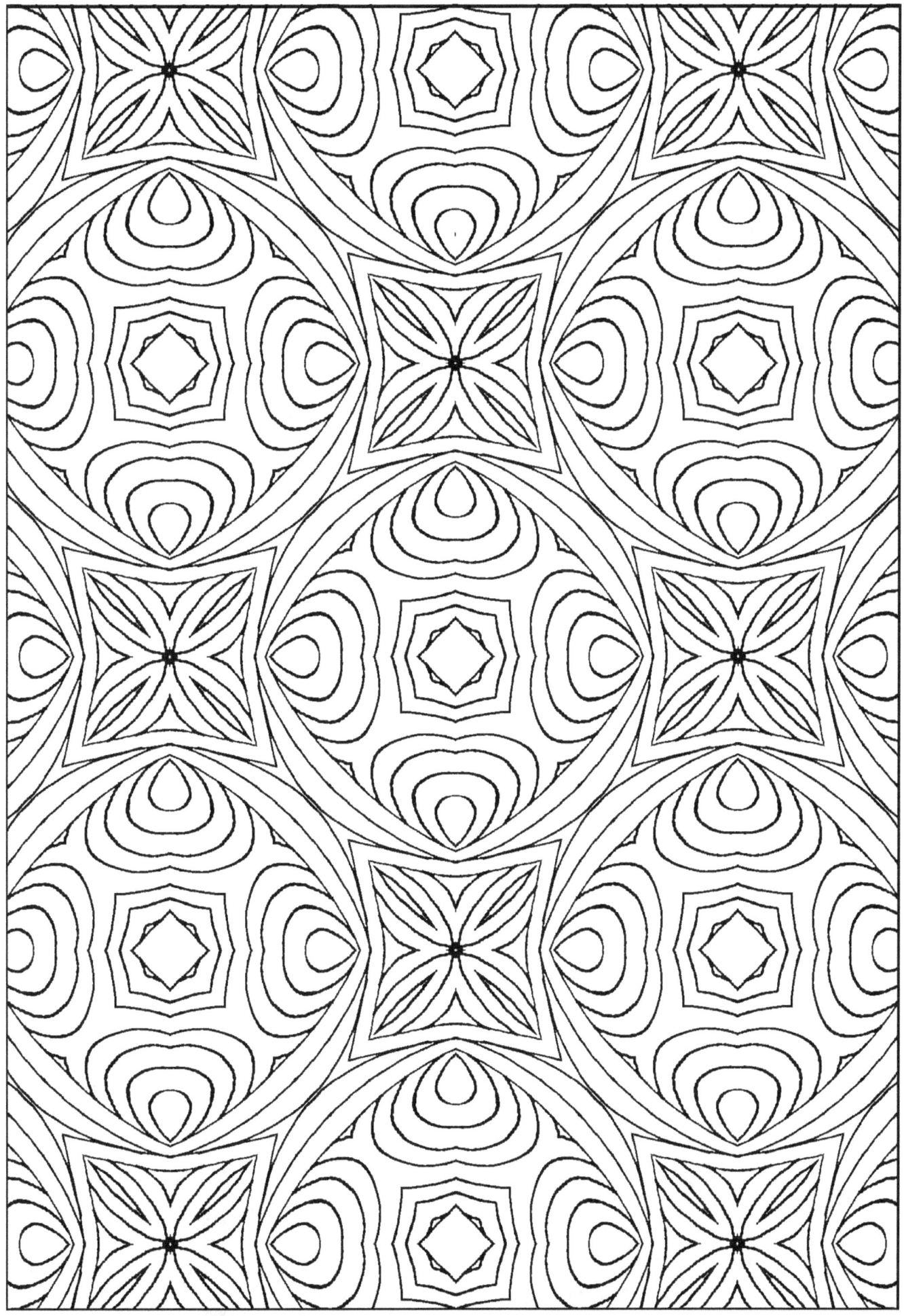

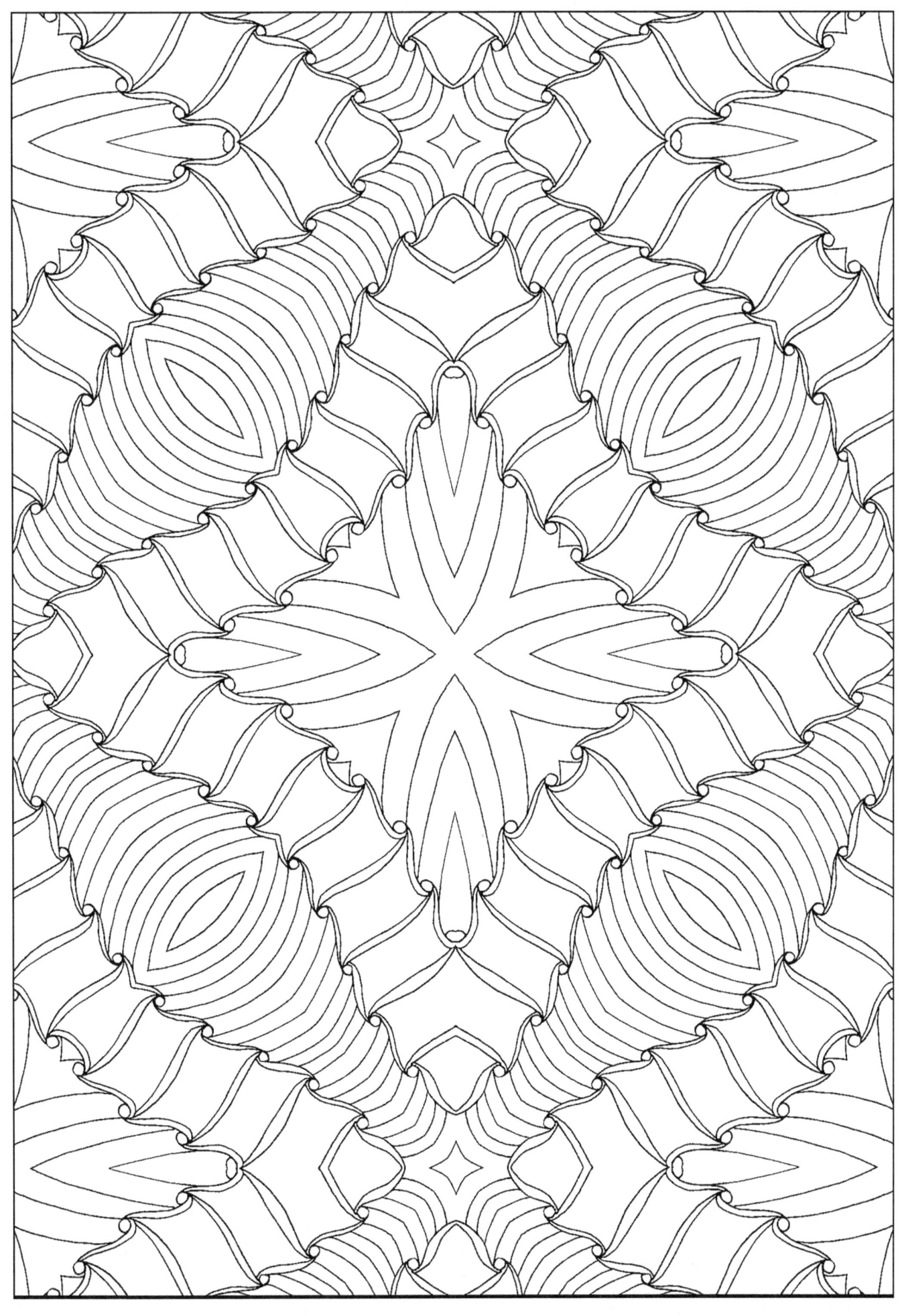

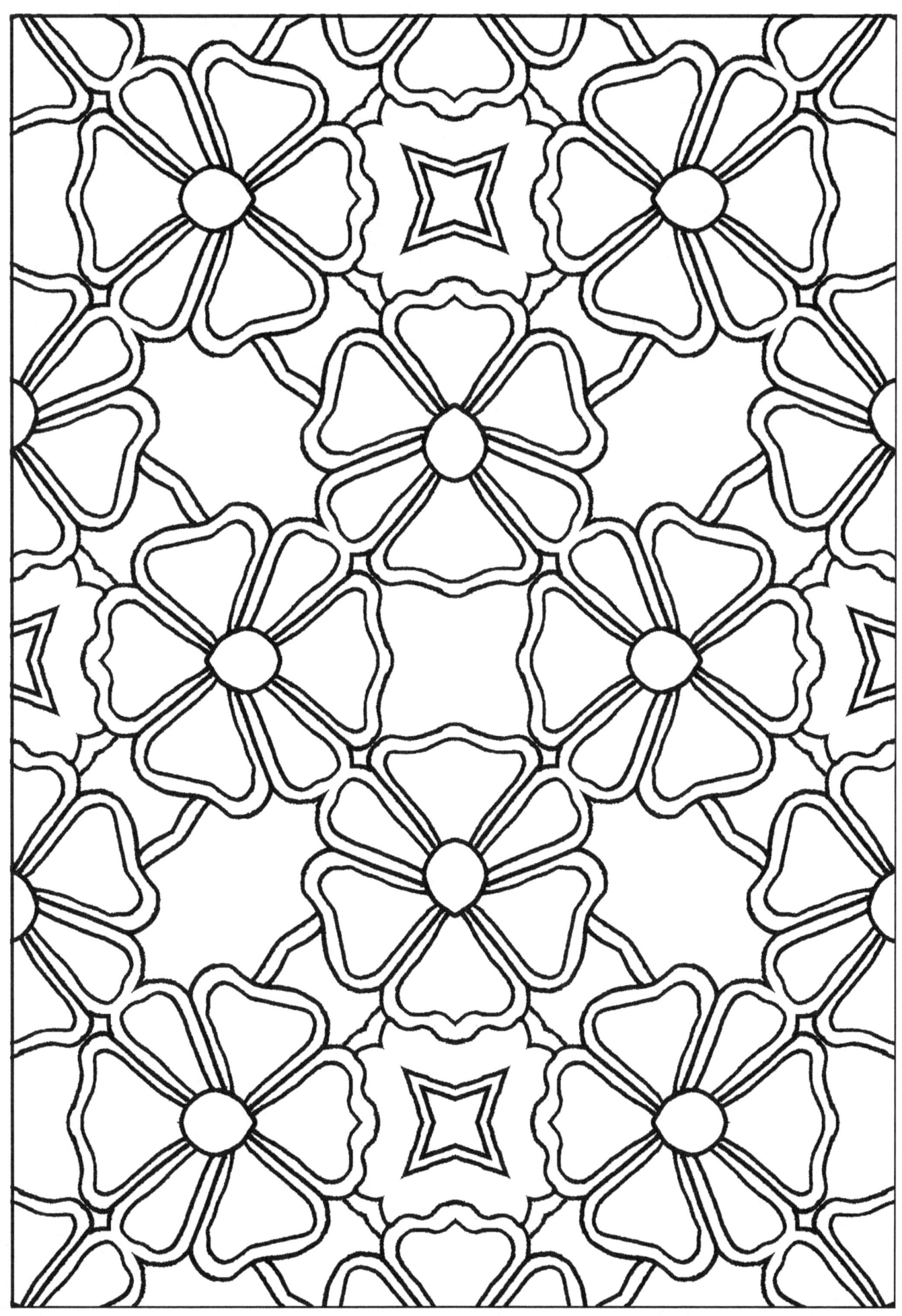

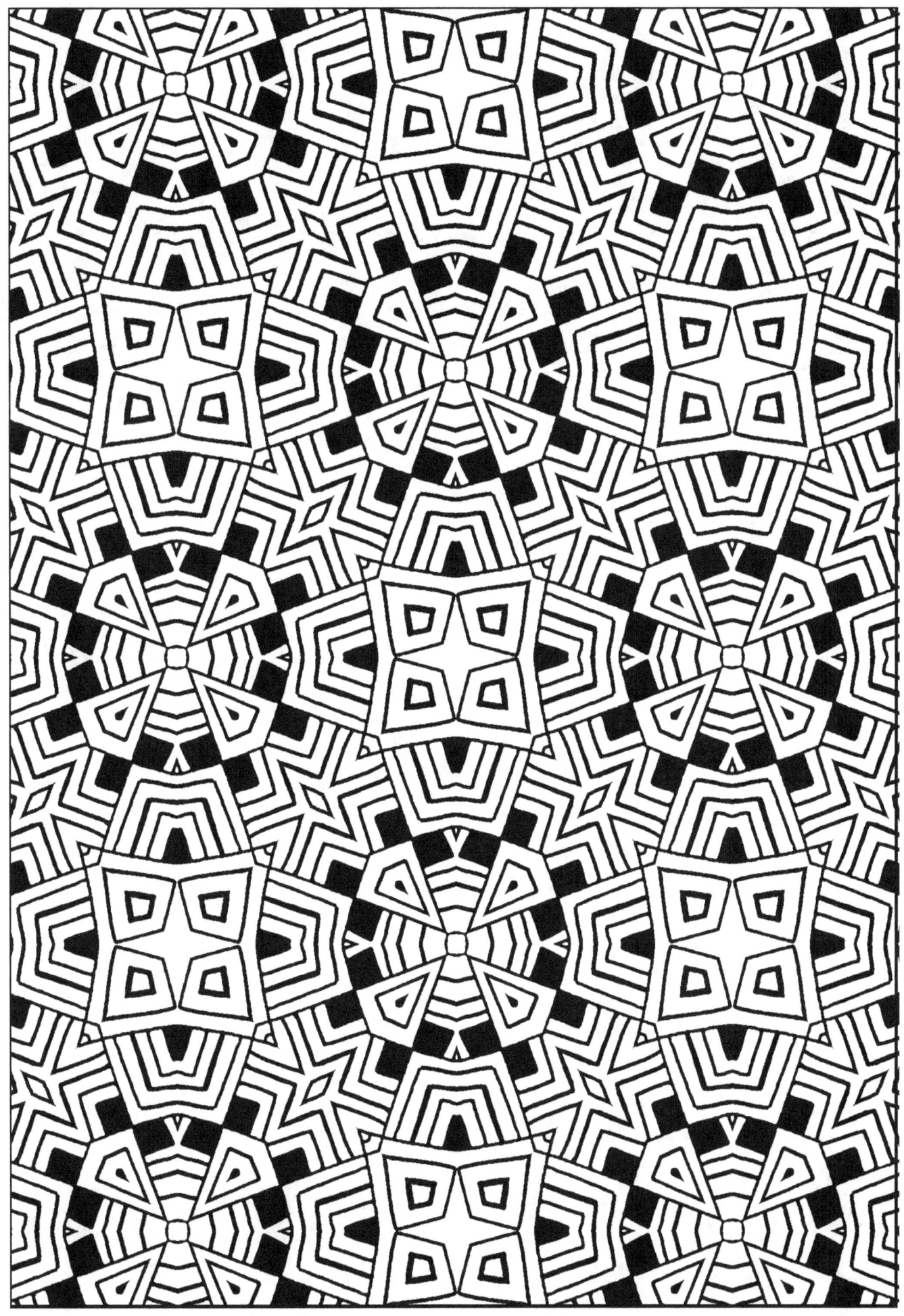

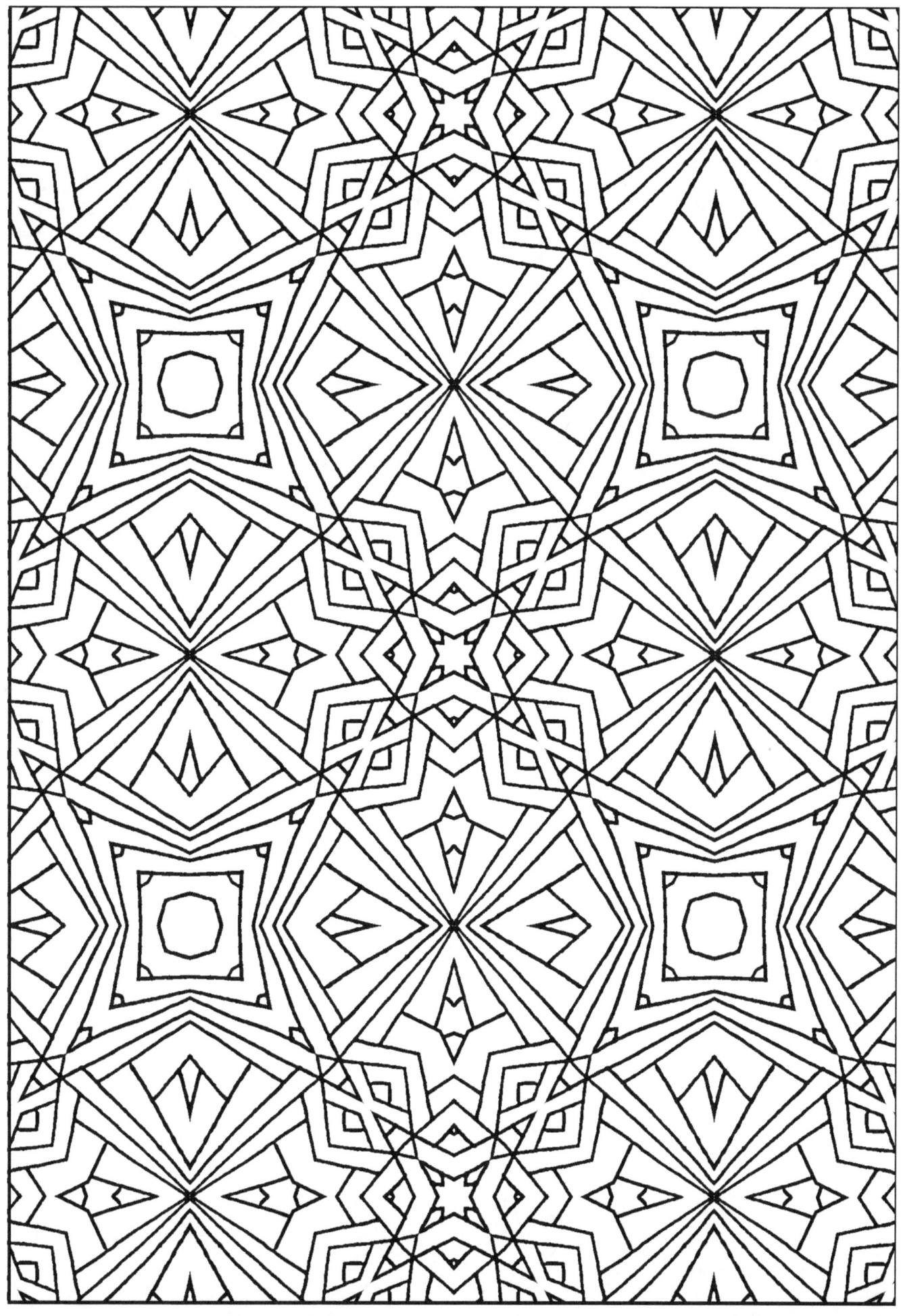

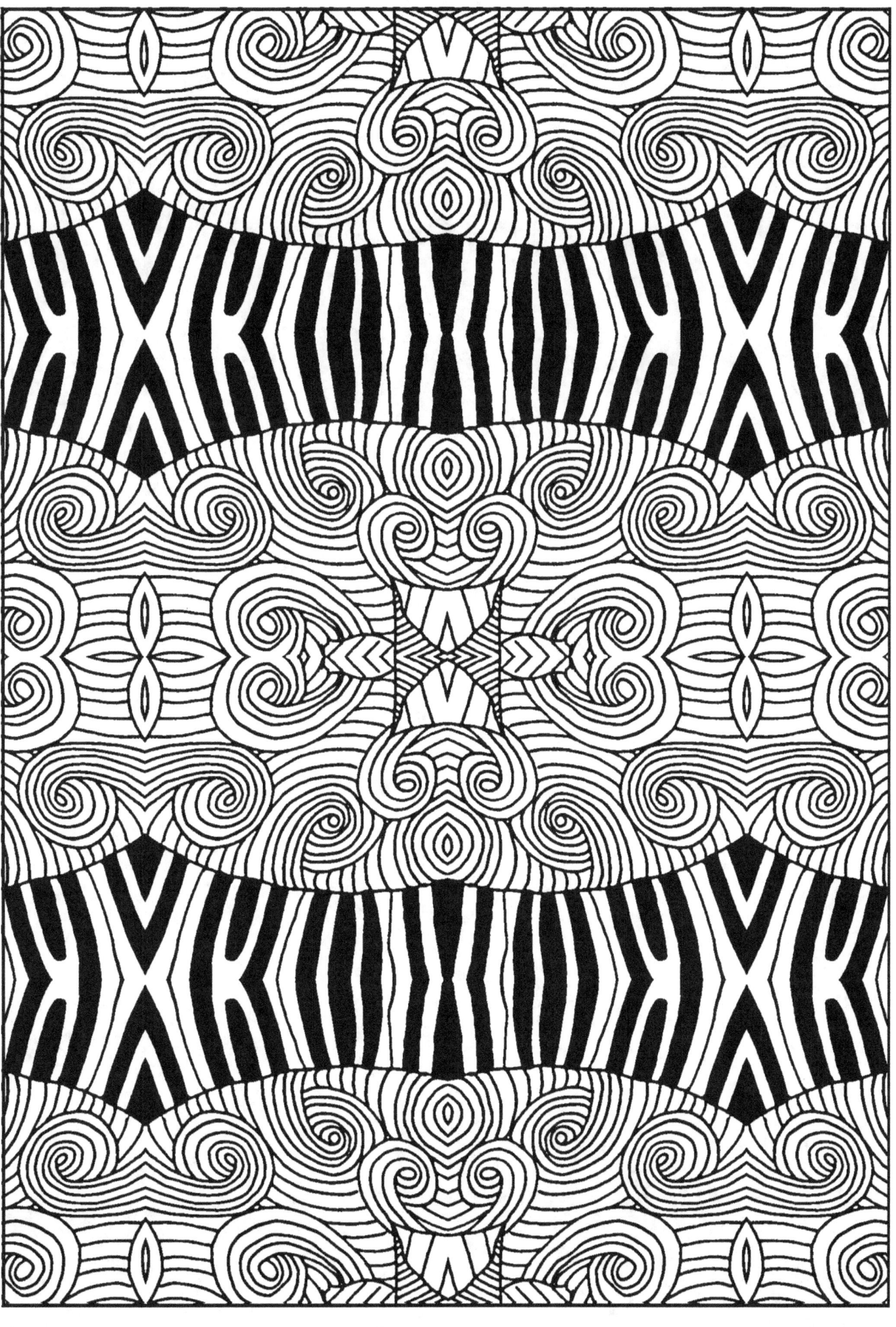

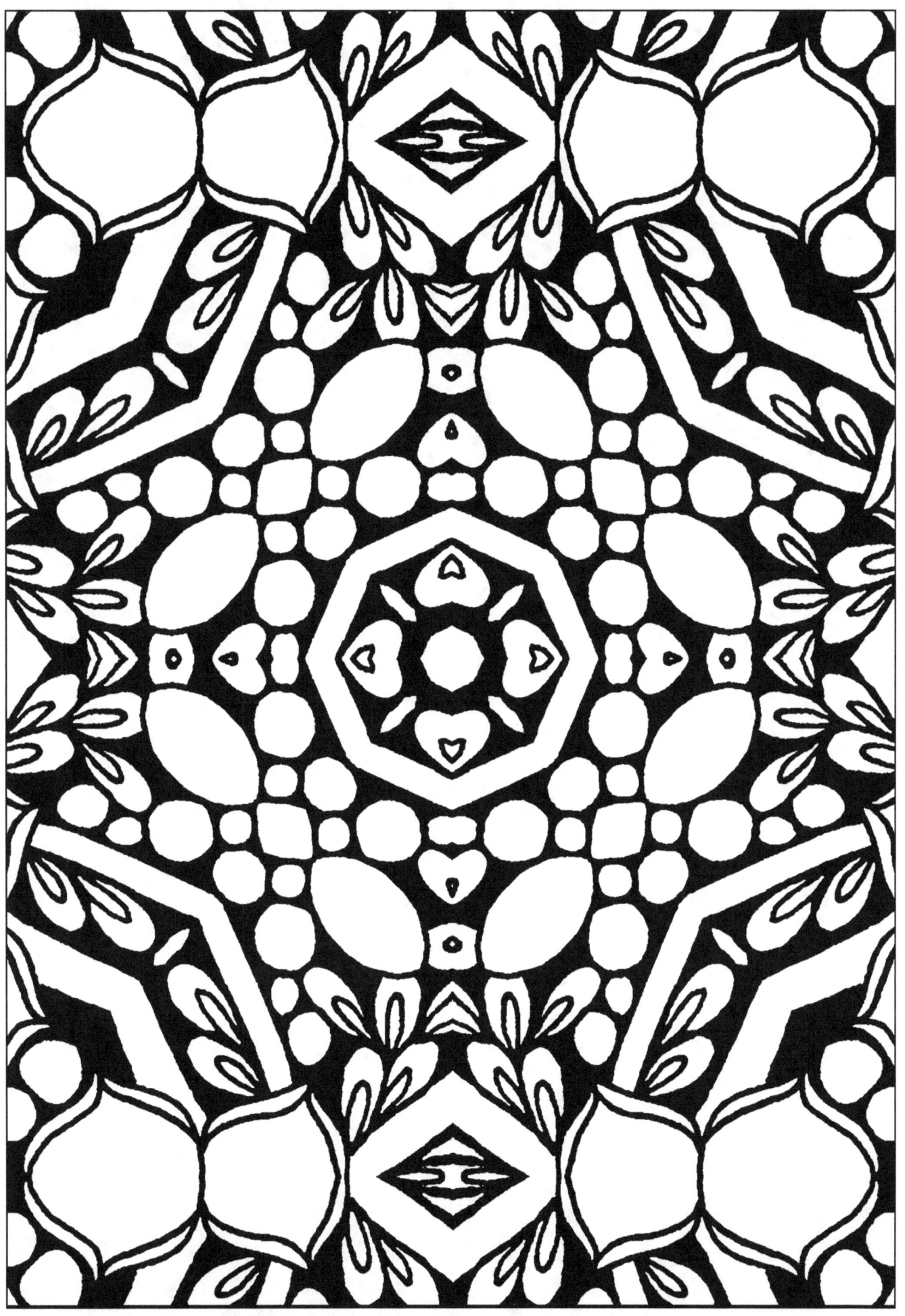

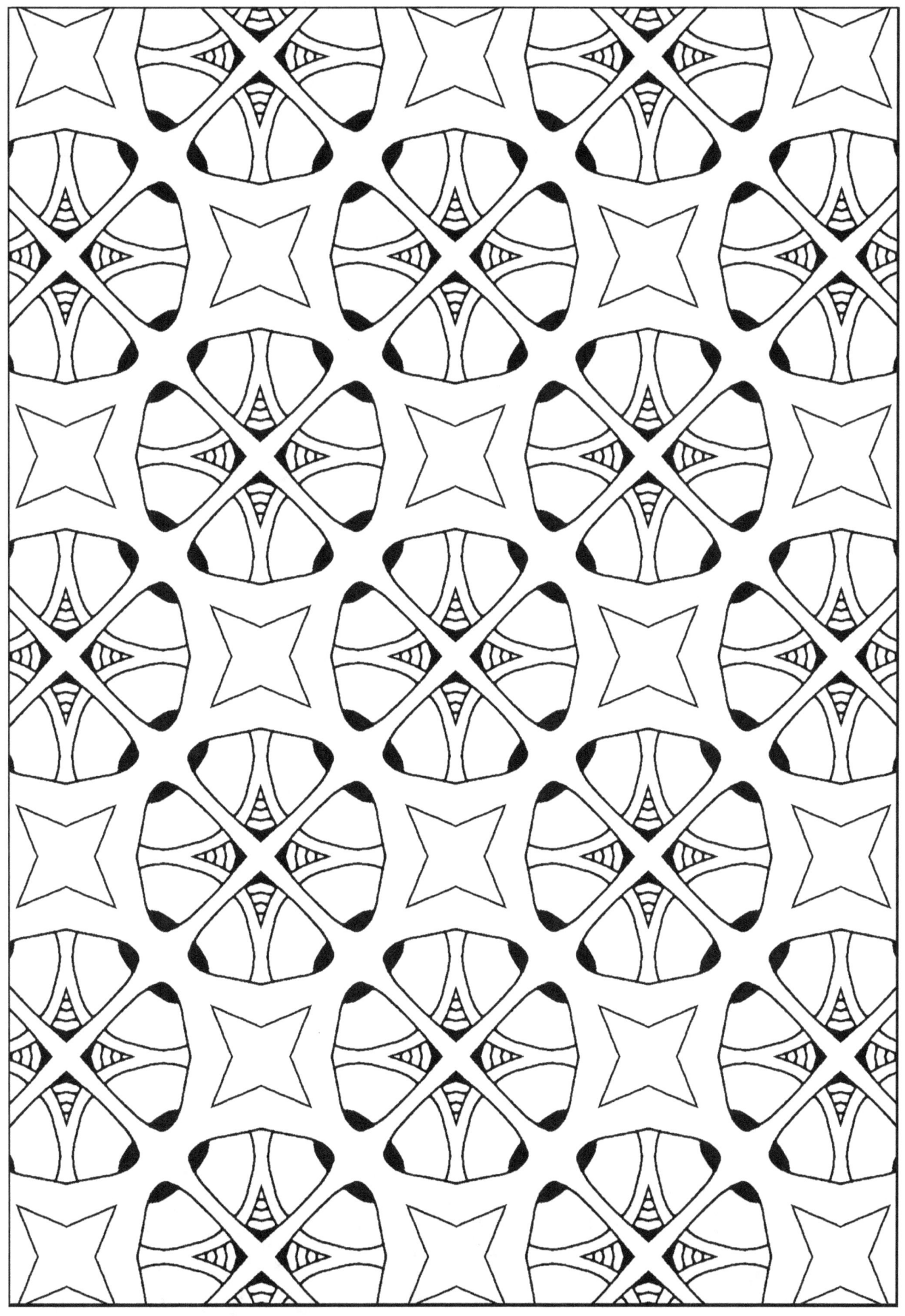

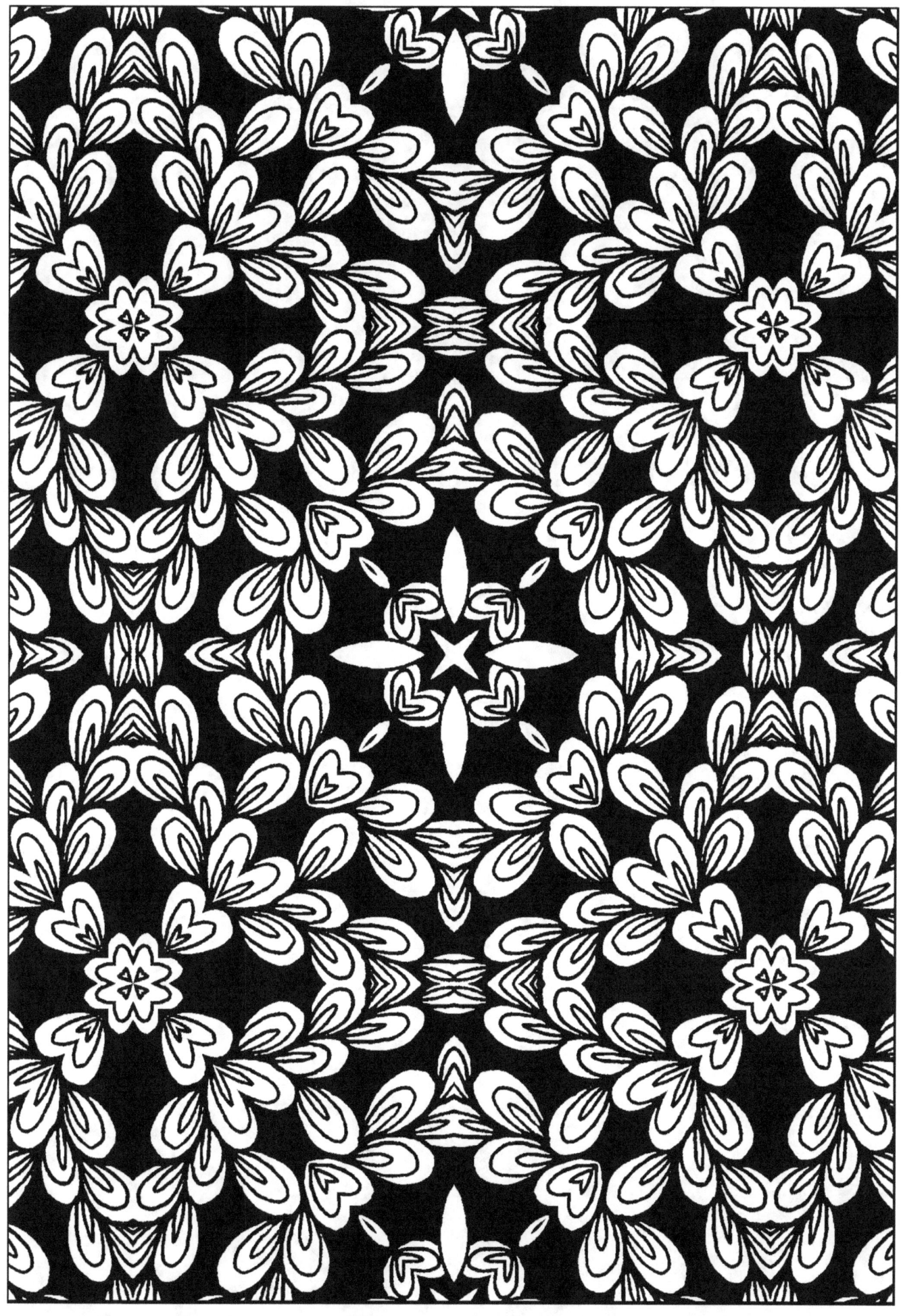

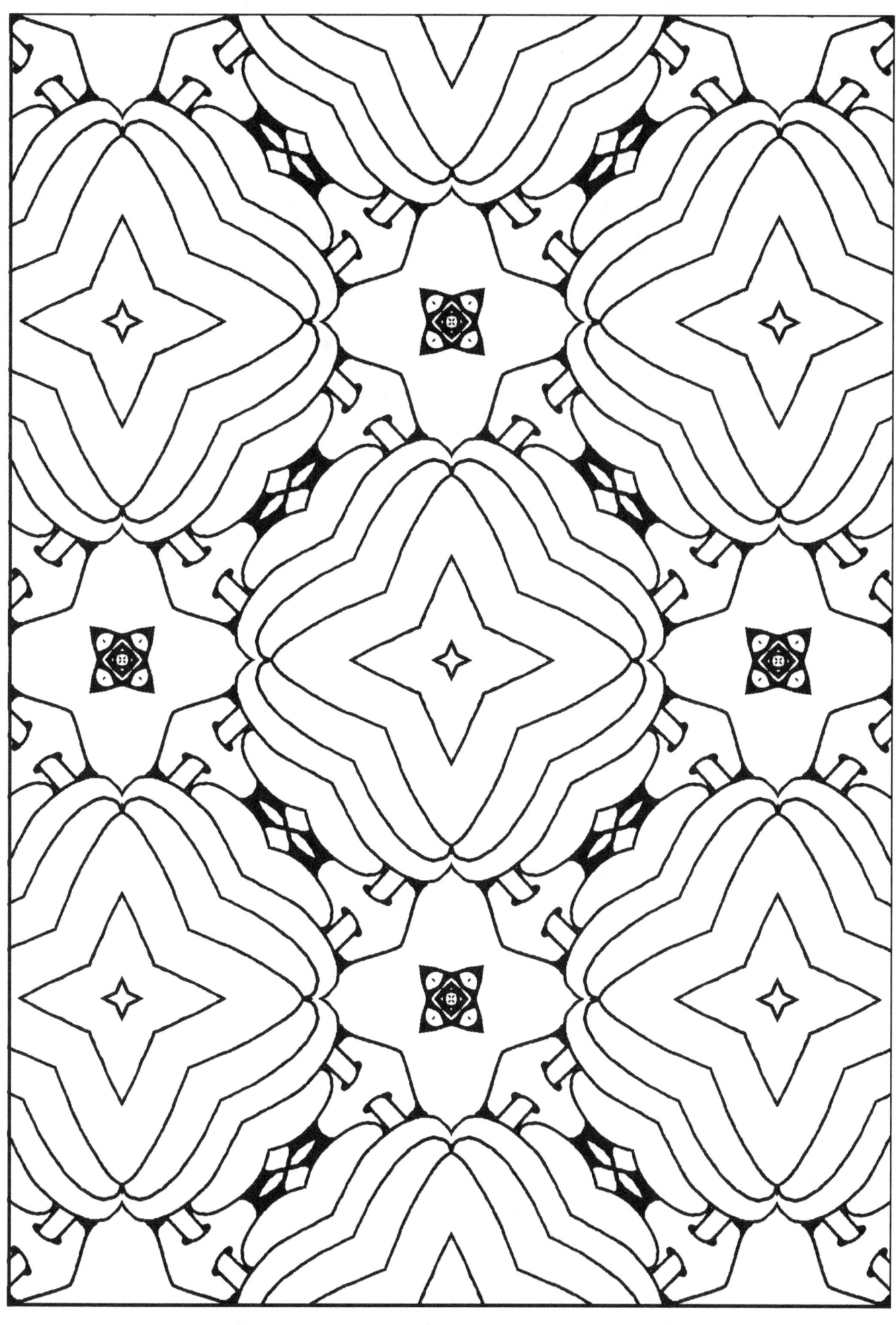

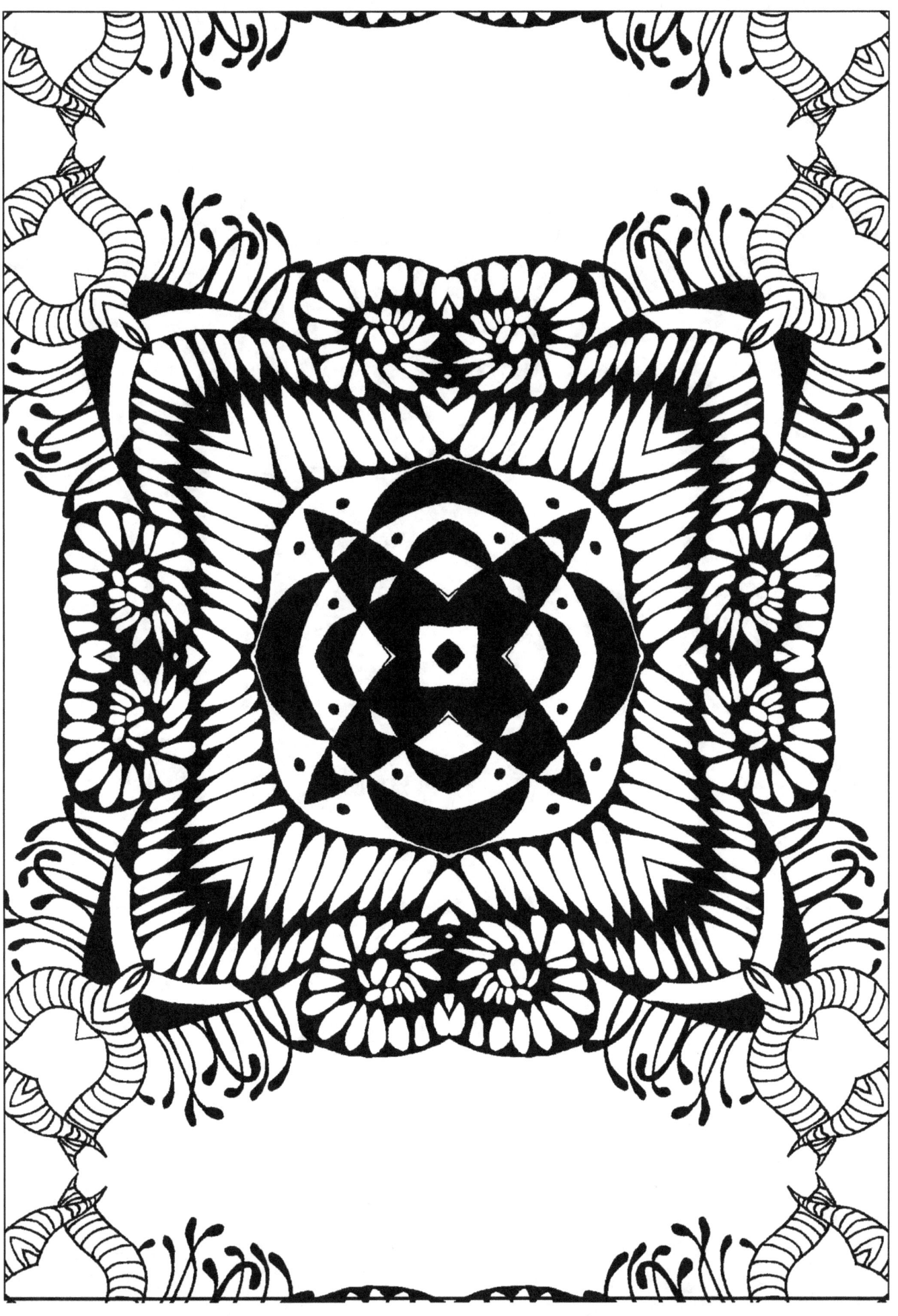

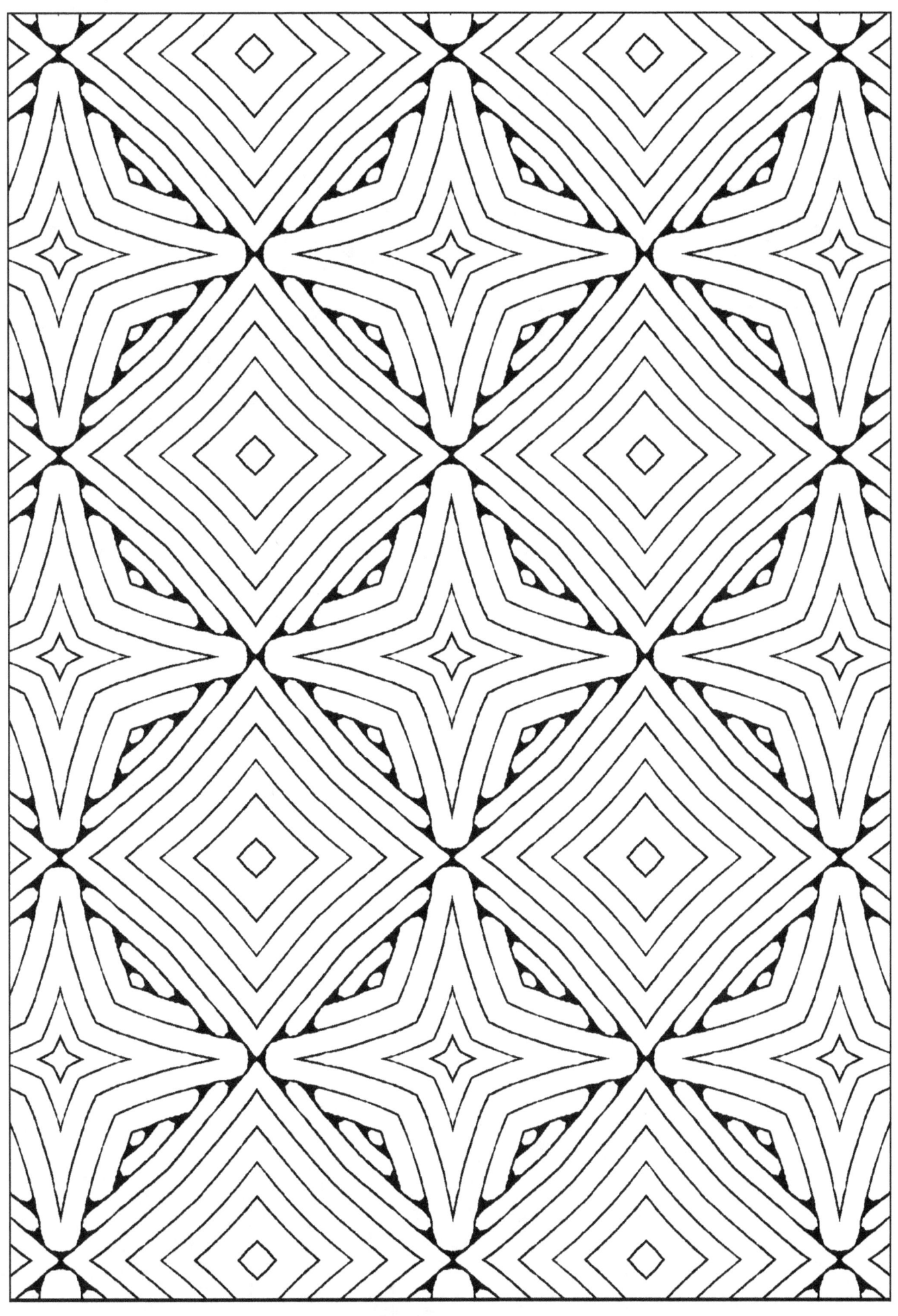

Blank Page

Remove and Insert Between
Pages if Using Wet Media

Blank Page

Remove and Insert Between
Pages if Using Wet Media

Blank Page

Remove and Insert Between
Pages if Using Wet Media

www.ingramcontent.com/pod-product-compliance
Lightning Source LLC
Chambersburg PA
CBHW080828180526
45168CB00006B/2609